Chi, and healing words from an ancient language.

"In the beginning was the word... John 1 vs. 1.

Chi, and healing words from an ancient language.

Understand Africa, Understand your world.

Uzoma Nwosu, MD

New York, New York.

Chi, and healing words from an ancient language.
Note to the reader; this book is not intended as a substitute for medical advice or treatment.

I recommend that you have a dictionary handy. Always check up any word you do not fully understand in any Standard English dictionary.

Table of Contents

Chi, and healing words from an ancient language.

Chi, and healing words from an ancient language.

ACKNOWLEDGEMENTS.

Many thanks to my parents, my grandparents, Igbo predecessors and all the authors who have contributed to human knowledge.

Chi, and healing words from an ancient language.

PURPOSE

The main purpose of this book is to introduce the world to the Chi, and the ancient people that created the Igbo language. This book demonstrates how these people considered their world, and how they drew conclusions from their environment.

Attempts were made to standardize the 'meaning' of objects, and phenomenon occurring in their world. When they encountered a rock, they tried to give it a meaning that is related to its practical purpose. This is a useful approach to life because it empowers us to create our own meanings and purposes. When we realize that an object like a rock does not have a specific purpose, it gives us the power to create our own additional uses of a rock. This is the power to create.

Language can be regarded as a form of communication technology between people. The aim of this book is to stimulate interest in the Chi, and the Igbo language, to ensure that the full potential of the language, and the embedded technology, is realized.

In addition, the author hopes that more people will come to;

- Know the Chi.
- Know Igbo language technology.
- Realize the accuracy of the language.
- Teach people the full potential of the language.
- Apply the language correctly.
- Encourage others to use the language and the embedded technology.
- Point out the incorrect use of the language and embedded technology.
- Remove incorrect use of the language and the embedded technology.
- Eliminate any possibility that the language and technology would be lost.
- Close the door to the incorrect use of the language and the technology.

Chi, and healing words from an ancient language.

PREFACE

There is considerable genetic, archeological, and paleontological evidence that language, most probably first developed, during the middle stone age, in sub-Saharan Africa. It is however unclear, how these early languages transformed into our current complex language systems.

One of the earliest challenges man faced was communication. Man needed to device a language that is easy to comprehend and accurate enough to transfer information from one person to another without loss of meaning. To come up with varying vocal sounds that convey accurate messages was, obviously, daunting. These sounds were obviously fashioned, and re-fashioned, over hundreds to thousands of years, in parallel with human development, to reach a level of complexity that endured the test of time. Accurate language systems create better communication between users, and increase their functional outcome in work and relationships.

We can assume that communities that employed good language systems would flourish more than those who do not. Language is an important index of survival in any community.

Language allows individuals to express their internal and external experiences. Words can be used to capture the truth about the observations a people make in their physical and spiritual world. By looking at each word, we could be examining their 'truth' as they have observed it.

I undertook this assignment after the realization that ancient Igbo words contain certain commands or actions in them. As I further examined the words, I began to realize that these words must have been created by a very complex ancient civilization. This civilization must have been more complex than what we know about Igbo culture today. Most importantly, I concluded that the examination of these words have great relevance in the modern world.

We can use the word for law which we all know as 'Iwu' to make a demonstration. The root word in 'Iwu' (law) can readily be identified as '**wu**'. But what is '**wu**'? To understand what that root '**wu**' communicates, let's look at other words containing the same root. One is o**wu**, which is used to describe the agony or distress an individual experiences when they are short

Chi, and healing words from an ancient language.
of money or funds. The other word is n**wu**te which is long suffering or prolonged agony an individual can experience due to a number of conditions. Notice that the verb '**te**' in nwu**te** is communicating a 'prolonged' event. So we can translate that verb **wu** as agony or distress. We will find out later that the '**I**' in **I**wu is a root or verb intensifier. So we can translate **I**wu(law) as **agonizing**.

In Igbo speech, when an individual violates the law, we say 'Iwu a ma go gi' which actually reads 'the law has known you' or 'agony has known you'. So the 'internal action' experienced by breaking the law is agony.

These words are communicated by the same root or verb for a specific purpose. When one breaks the law (i**wu**), not only would there be agony; there would be o**wu** (agony due to lack of funds/means), and then n**wu**te (prolonged suffering). The purpose is synergism.

Interest in the origin of words is rising. The word hippopotamus is actually of ancient Greek origin from hippos-potamios, literally, riverine horse. This clarification helps us understand when the ancient Greeks first encountered and named this animal, and how it eventually became an English word.

In the modern world, we tend to revere ancient man-made structures such as the pyramids of Egypt and Nubia that have survived for thousands of years. Unfortunately, languages that have survived besides those structures have not attracted considerable admiration.

This work is intended to demonstrate how parts of the language were built, and why it has survived thousands of years till this day.

Understanding Igbo words, their origin, and what they communicate is believed to add to our wisdom, and help us act more effectively in our universe.

Chi, and healing words from an ancient language.

<u>INTRODUCTION</u>

The Igbo people are one of the most prominent ethnic groups in Africa with a primary homeland in the South Eastern area of Nigeria. Igbos are one of the largest and powerful ethnic groups in Nigeria. If the Igbos had their own country, they would have a population size that would exceed many African countries.
The Igbos also live in surrounding countries, most notably Cameroun, Gabon and Equatorial Guinea.
They constitute significant numbers in many countries around the world especially the United States, the United Kingdom and other major economic hubs of the world.
Obviously, one important 'help' that allowed them to flourish in Africa Is the language.
Igbo (the language) is tonal and verb based. In other words, Igbo is an action based language. Each word is intended to convey a certain action or motion. But because a thought or spirit always precedes any given action, Igbo can be considered a spiritual language.

In this work, we are performing etymological analysis of Igbo words. By looking at the components or roots of each word; we are looking at the action or motion a word conveys. We are also looking at the spirit(or thought)before each word.
The Igbo language was designed to create a system of communication that enables individuals participate and gain competence in their environment by matching words with certain actions. This creates a system of communication that allows individuals to express themselves without the use of force.

The words are arranged like a tree. Verbs are used to create word branches carrying closely related words.
For example, the verb '**wu**' carries such words such as i**wu** (law), O**wu** (agony), e**wu** (goat), and n**wu**te (prolonged agony).

Chi, and healing words from an ancient language.

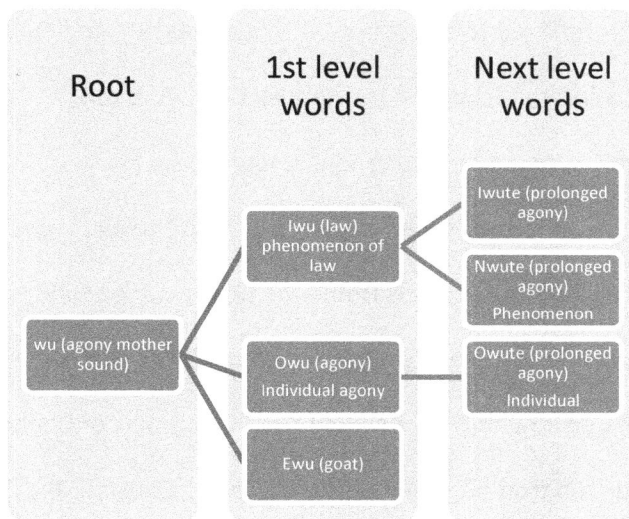

Root	1st level words	Next level words
wu (agony mother sound)	Iwu (law) phenomenon of law	Iwute (prolonged agony)
		Nwute (prolonged agony) Phenomenon
	Owu (agony) Individual agony	Owute (prolonged agony) Individual
	Ewu (goat)	

Igbo word tree showing the root word for agony 'wu'.

This work is intended to provide you with the skeleton of the system.

The word Igbo was derived from 'I' (a prefix used as a verb/noun intensifier) and 'gbo'(prevent, guard). The verb or action word here is to guard. Originally the Igbo's were intended to be guards.

At the time of writing, it is not clear to most people what the Igbo were guarding, or if they lost something they were supposed to protect. Through this work, I will endeavor to provide you with a glimpse.

In this work, the Onitsha dialect is used. The author is only fluent in the Onitsha dialect. Onitsha is an important trading post and was once the largest single market in West Africa.

Chi, and healing words from an ancient language.

IGBO SPIRITUALITY

Igbo spirituality is monotheistic with a central God called 'Chukwu'.

The religion is referred to as odinani (within the earth), and contains

technology to create success on this planet. Chukwu is too

powerful to be engaged directly, and is served by several

smaller intermediary gods called 'Alụsi'. Each Alụsi, covers a given area

of life on earth. Alụsi was coined from 'Alụ' (abomination) and 'si' (stop).

Each individual possesses a personal force called 'Chi' that helps

determine the destiny of the individual. The 'Chi' is part of Chukwu (God).

Chukwu is derived from 'Chi' & ukwu (big) making Chukwu (Big Chi).

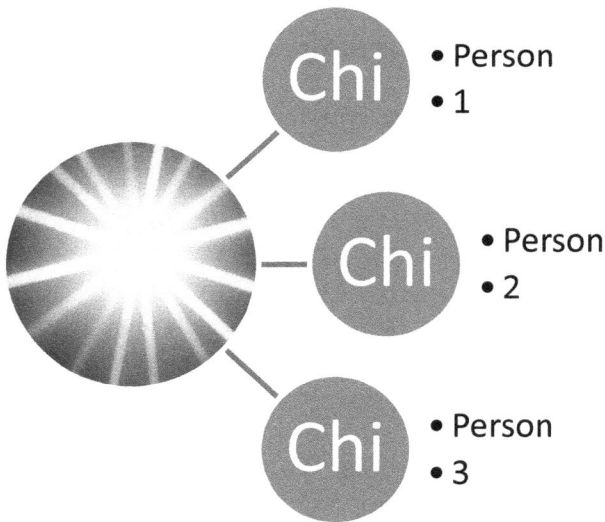

- Person
- 1

- Person
- 2

- Person
- 3

God (Chukwu) is the Big Chi

Chi, and healing words from an ancient language.
Chi can be regarded as an individual's spiritual guardian, and is believed to

be responsible for the individuals failures and successes.

These four phrases are readily used in everyday Igbo speech and help

define Chi;

- "**Chi** mụ egbu o mụ" (my **Chi** has killed/failed me) is often expressed when an individual experiences a misfortune.
- "Onye kwe **Chi** ya ekwe" (when one agrees his/her **Chi** agrees)

   is a positive statement that suggests individuals have some

   control over their **Chi**.

- Further, the expression 'maka **Chi**' (because of **Chi**) is often made

   as justification for a future retaliatory action. This suggests that an

   individual could take actions to protect his/her **Chi**.

- In addition, **Chi** mụ mụ anya (my **Chi** is awake) is a statement made

   when danger or destruction is averted, and demonstrates that

   alertness is one of the features of the **Chi**.

Chi is, simply, the summation of an individual's emotional and spiritual

force. It is an emotional complex of the spirit, soul and body

(including diseases) of an individual.

When the Chi contains a predominance of love, joy, happiness and other

positive emotions, life results are favorable. On the other hand, when the

chi contains jealousy, anxiety, depression, revenge and other

negative emotions, misfortunes are bound to happen.

Chi, and healing words from an ancient language.

We know that God (Big Chi) is Spirit and Love, so we can readily extrapolate that Chi is an individual's spiritual force that contains (or should contain) love. Love is a pure emotion that is characterized by high quality thoughts and the greatest abilities (God is omnipotent). One sure way to fail in life is to replace love with anger, depression, frustration, prejudice, jealousy, fear, anxiety, or any other negative emotion.

We know from Biblical sources that 'we are nothing without love' and 'love is the greatest' (1 Corinthians 13). Igbo cultural activities is replete with love boosting activities such as games, music, and dancing around an open fire. The aim is to boost the love people have for themselves and others.

Interestingly, according to Chinese culture; the chi (qi) is a type of energy and life force, and is the central underlying principle of Chinese Medicine. The subject of the 'Chi' is well known in Chinese martial arts and in acupuncture.

Eri is regarded as the cultural head of the Igbo people. Oral and recorded accounts suggest he is a sky being, having been sent down to earth by God. It has been suggested that Eri was an extra-terrestrial.

Chi, and healing words from an ancient language.

ETYMOLOGY OF IGBO WORDS.

It is likely that the Igbos had a 'mother sound' from which they created words from. Although, we may not readily find this sound, we can readily access words that have survived till this day that were created out of more 'primitive' sounds.

Igbo words are, commonly, derivatives and fusion of other verbs or words. These words were engineered to resonate with each other, resonate with words for verbs and nouns in the physical and spiritual plane, to the extent that the power of the individual words are amplified. We can describe this phenomenon as synergism. We can also consider it a form of neuro-linguistics.

The intention is to create a highly effective community were harmony is achieved by the spoken word rather than whips, police or prisons.

A, e, o, i, u , n, ọ, ụ, are prefixes used to propel/amplify/intensify a root verb or a noun to varying degrees of intensity.

They are commonly placed before a noun/verb, but can also be placed after, as suffixes, as in di or du.

Prefix	Use
'a'	is used to create the negative of the verb or noun. It is similar to the alpha derivative of ancient Greek. E.g. geometry and ageometry (without geometry). 'à' is negative 'a.' It can also be used in a neutral manner in front of a verb or noun. When used in this context, it can serve as an abbreviation of 'I am' or 'anyi' (we).
'e'	is used to muffle the power of a verb or noun or create a partial positive or a partial negative. In egwu (fear) the 'e' is a partial negative. In egwu (game), it is a partial positive.
'I'	is a verb/noun intensifier used to create a strong positive.
'U'	is a verb/noun intensifier often when referring to a group of people(community).
'N'	is a verb/noun intensifier, often used as a positive prefix in phenomenon.
'O'	is used personally as an intensifier.
'ọ'	is used personally as an intensifier.
'ụ'	Is used in community or multiple person settings.

Chi, and healing words from an ancient language.

In some cases, there are slight phonological differences between nouns and verbs. The principle of approximation is used in these cases, e.g. the earth is not a true sphere but acts like one. So when NASA scientists make calculations regarding the earth they use sphere equations, and it checks out right. This is how approximation works.

These phonological differences could be explained because the events occur in either the physical or spiritual plane. A good example is the verb 'we' which is used to communicate the concept of withdrawal in the physical plane. Now a phonologically very similar verb 'we' is found in the word for anger 'Iwe'. This is because anger is basically withdrawal, but this 'withdrawal' occurs spiritually or mentally. The reason you cannot speak or communicate with an angry person is that the real person has 'withdrawn'. What is left in charge is an 'incomplete' being, and this explains the weird behavior associated with anger.

Let's begin!

Chi, and healing words from an ancient language.

THE WORDS

Celestial bodies and their manifestations

English:	Sun
Igbo:	Anwụ
Break down: 'a' (negative prefix) & 'nwụ'(die)	
Comments: 'a' creates the negative-that which does not die. The sun does not die, slumber or sleep. The sun is not like humans whose physical bodies' live and die. The sun represents happiness because it always achieves its goals. It is steadfast, always rising in the morning, and setting at night. It encourages us to start our daily activities at sunrise, and wrap things up at sunset. Sometimes the weather prevents the sun from shining bright on earth, but it is not deterred. It steadfastly rises and sets every day until the weather improves. It is a model which we may follow in our endeavors. We should never give up due to unfavorable circumstances. The sun allows us to introduce a very important concept in ancient igbo- anyanwụ (eye of the sun). We are encouraged to develop an 'eye for the sun'. We may notice the sun as we leave our houses, and as we go about our daily activities. Noting what position the sun is in the sky. Whether it is at the 11 or 3.00 o'clock position, as examples. The sun consciousness is expected to increase our alignment with the sun, and keep us more balanced. It also allows us to juxtaposition our intentions, with that of the sun. The Igbo know the earth turns around itself and the sun, hence the statement; "ụwa na eme ntụ hari".	

Chi, and healing words from an ancient language.

English:	Moon
Igbo:	ọnwa
Breakdown:	'ọ'(prefix)& 'nwa' (child)
Comments:	The moon as a child of the earth. The moon is a breakaway piece of the earth. The moon is also like a child. It starts small as the new moon, and then grows to its full size, before fading. This transient and mobile nature of the moon gives us a perspective when we deal with our children. We have to understand that our relationship with our children is like the earth and the moon. We can influence our children, but they have a degree of autonomy.

English:	Star
Igbo:	Kpakpando
Breakdown:	Kpa X 2 (ruffle, scatter, border, burden) & ' ndo'(shade, shield, canopy, roof)
Comments:	That which scatters the shield or shade. It is believed that the sky and the clouds are a shield or shade that protects the earth from the powerful rays of the sun and stars(see also ozone layer). The light of the stars are powerful enough to scatter that shield and hence their light reaches us as stars (kpakpando). Without the shield, there will be no night as the light from billions of stars will illuminate the earth at night. The sun is powerful enough to penetrate the shield completely and produce daylight. Sunset provides a powerful illustration of the power of the ndo (the sky and the clouds). Notice that the sky and clouds are able to shield us from the power of the sun at sunset to the point that we can gaze at the sun. This is impossible at mid-day. For a while after sunset, the sky illuminates from the energy it trapped from the sun (in much the same way as the leaves of a tree trap light). The energy is released as light, and the beautiful coloring is a function of the gases illuminated. When much of the light energy is dispensed, the light of the stars become powerful enough to 'ruffle', break through the sky and clouds and reach us as kpakpando.

Chi, and healing words from an ancient language.

Without the 'shade', the light from trillions of stars would keep the earth illuminated at night.

English:	Sky, heavens.
Igbo:	Enu
Breakdown:	'e'(partial positive) & 'nu'(nudge, push)
Comments:	That which nudges or motivates. A gentle push. 'e' is a muffler (partial positive) in this case. Want to get motivated; always look up. On the earth, there are numerous people and objects that can obstruct our progress. Not so up there, it is quite expansive. This is why the spirit feels better when it looks up.

Chi, and healing words from an ancient language.

English:	Dawn
Igbo:	Chi-efo
Breakdown:	'Chi' (end) & 'e' (partial positive prefix) & 'fo' (withdraw)
Comments:	The contrast between day and night is very significant. Night was considered the end of the day. Obviously this is an end that is relatively long lasting because it lingers for several hours. When this end 'withdraws' we have day break.

English:	Dawn
Igbo:	ụzọ (ụzọ ụtụtụ)
Breakdown:	'ụ' (community prefix) & 'zọ' (save)
Comments:	Being active at dawn is a way to 'save' the day. People who wake up before or at sunrise can have a very productive day.

English:	Morning
Igbo:	ụtụtụ
Breakdown:	'ụ' (prefix used in community settings) and 'tụtụ' (pick up)
Comments:	When the sun rises in the morning, it can be quite beautiful. A new day has begun and it is time to 'pick up' the things we need to do for the day. For some, it may be to 'pick up' herbs, such as mint and sarsaparilla, that can be used to make healthy tea, or sweep the leaves that have fallen off the trees, or it may be to pick up your book and study, or to 'pick up' raw food and cook. For those who love tea or coffee it might be reaching out and 'picking up' your next cup. The use of u (the community prefix) suggests that whatever you have to 'pick up' in the morning, we need to keep an eye on the community role of our activities.

Chi, and healing words from an ancient language.

English:	Day (in the past)
Igbo:	ụbọsi
Breakdown:	'ụ' (community prefix) & 'bọ' (dig) & 'si' (stop)
Comments:	This word is often used to describe an event that happened on a day in the past. In an agricultural society, most people spend their active days digging mounds or digging out weeds. Social events tend to happen on days or periods when there is no digging. This is why ụbọsi (digging stopped) is used. Further, Igbo has a lunar calendar and the days could have been counted at night when there is no farm work.

English:	Afternoon
Igbo:	Efifie
Breakdown:	'e' (partial positive prefix)& fi (massage) & fi (massage) & 'e' (suffix used as a partial positive).
Comments:	The verb 'fi' is seen in the word to clean 'fi-cha' where it means 'rub (massage) clean'. It is also in the word for 'rub' as 'fia'. The sun picks us up in the morning and gives us gentle 'massages' in the afternoon. The afternoon represents the peak of the work day. The sun nudges us along. It is time to start cleaning up our days work.

English:	Evening
Igbo:	Mgbede
Breakdown:	'mgbe' (time, period) &' de' (straighten, make right)
Comments:	The verb 'de' is used in ironing (clothing) because it conveys the notion of making right or straightening. The evening is a time to make things right. Time to start wrapping up the activities of the day in anticipation of night fall and a new day. This is also a time to refresh the spirit. Games and dances often occur in the evening, and allow people the opportunity to re-make the day. In the modern world, people go to movies, dinner, or after work drinks, as part of a way to remake the day after hard-work.

Chi, and healing words from an ancient language.

English:	Dusk, darkness
Igbo:	Chi- ji
Breakdown:	'chi' (end) & 'ji' (holding)
Comments:	The day is very important because of all the things we can achieve when the sun is out. When it comes to an end, darkness prevails. This darkness lasts several hours until the next day, and is considered to be a time when the 'end is holding'. The verb 'ji' is also used for dark or black because dark or black objects or phenomenon are 'holding' something.

English:	Night
Igbo:	Abani
Breakdown:	'a'(negative prefix) & 'ba'(enter) & 'ani'(land)
Comments:	Night as a time not to venture into the farm, land or town. Be watchful of dangerous people and animals.

English:	Night
Igbo:	Anyasi
Breakdown:	'anya'(eye) & 'si'(stop)
Comments:	Time to close the eyes. Night as time to rest the eyes. This allows the brain to adjust from the entire stimulus it receives while the eyes are open.

English:	Night (late night)
Igbo:	uchichi
Breakdown:	'u' (community prefix) &'chi' (end) & chi (end)
Comments:	Darkness signals the end of the day. However, the end is only temporary. Late night represents the 'end of the end'. Night is a very important period because it indicates the end of the previous day. The next day is totally brand new and is not necessarily connected to the previous one. That's why we should endeavor to leave past events alone.

Chi, and healing words from an ancient language.

English:	Tomorrow
Igbo:	Echi
Breakdown:	'e' (partial negative) & 'chi' (end)
Comments:	Everyday has an end, and that is a complete end. We cannot remove or add to it, once it occurs. Tomorrow is marked by an 'unending' of the previous night.

English:	The day after tomorrow
Igbo:	Nwanne-echi
Breakdown:	'Nwanne' (sibling) & 'echi' (tomorrow)
Comments:	Although the sun rises every morning, each day can be quite different. Each day varies from the next, as much as a brother differs from a sister. So our days are not linked at all, they are completely different entities. This is why we should never let events from the past unduly influence us. Do not let past failures affect your ability to make decisions today or drag you into sadness today. The only day that is truly real, is the day we are in. The next ones are completely separate. This is why the Bible tells us to 'rejoice and be glad in the day that the Lord has made and never to worry about tomorrow'.

English:	The day before yesterday
Igbo:	Nwanne nnya
Breakdown:	'Nwanne' (sibling) & 'nnya' (yesterday)
Comments:	Each day is different as much as a sister differs from brother. See nwanne echi (the day after tomorrow).

English:	Month
Igbo:	ọnwa
Breakdown:	ọnwa=moon
Comments:	The Igbo have a lunar calendar based on a 4 day week. There are 7 weeks, and 28 days in a month. A year is made of 13 months. It takes the moon about 27.33 days to circle the earth (sidereal month). The length of time from new moon to new moon is 29.53 days (lunar month or synodic period).

The elements

English:	Earth
Igbo:	Ana
Breakdown:	'a' & 'na'(to go)
Comments:	'a' creates the negative; that which does not go away. The earth or land as something permanent. Our earth is permanent.

The earth, our playground, never goes away.

English:	Wind
Igbo:	Ikuku
Breakdown:	'I' (positive prefix) & 'ku' (to move air) & 'ku' (to move air)
Comments:	Wind is just repeated air movement. The verb ku is also used in 'carrying' because this activity also causes an air movement.

Chi, and healing words from an ancient language.

English:	Fire
Igbo:	ọkụ
Breakdown:	'ọ' (prefix) and 'kụ'(breakdown)
Comments:	Fire as that which breaks down! Be it food item or a house, etc.

English:	Hot
Igbo:	ọkụ
Breakdown:	'ọ' (prefix) and 'kụ'(breakdown)
Comments:	Heat is related to fire, and breaks down materials.

English:	Water
Igbo:	Mmiri
Breakdown:	'Mmi' (deep) + 'ri' (leak, reach out, flow).
Comments:	Water as deep flowing. Water is indispensable for survival and is truly deep flowing. When we drink water, it is quickly absorbed and distributed around the body. The same is true for water as rain, river, sea or ocean. It is deep flowing.

Deep flowing Niagra Falls. Image by D Mayer.

Chi, and healing words from an ancient language.

English:	Cold
Igbo:	Oyi
Breakdown:	'o' (personal prefix) & ' yi' (wear)
Comments:	Cold makes us wear clothing. See also yi (wear), and note that to wear clothing is a way to 'look like' the clothing you are wearing.

Places

English:	Hill
Igbo:	Ugwu
Breakdown:	'U' (community prefix) & 'gwu' (to build a protection)
Comments:	We use the verb 'gwu' to communicate the digging motion that creates a mound. The purpose of a mound is to protect a seed from the elements, and from seed eaters such as birds. So we can translate the verb 'gwu' as protection, making hill (ugwu) the creation of a protection. In early times, people often settled on hills because it provided protection against flood and fierce storms. A hill is also easier to defend compared to lower ground. Because the hill looks like a huge mound, it would appear it was created by a god or God. So the hill helped develop early beliefs in the existence of God. The mound is to the seed what the hill is to man-protection. So you can understand why the Psalmist says, 'I look up unto the hills, from whence does my help come' (Psalm 121).

Chi, and healing words from an ancient language.

English:	Farm
Igbo:	Ubi
Breakdown:	'U' (community prefix) & 'bi' (to live)
Comments:	A garden next to the house (Obi) is called an ubi. It often contains vegetables such as pumpkin leaves, garden eggs and tomatoes that are essential for healthy living. Having this type of farm, amounts to having a life in the community. An 'ubi' is not just uplifting spiritually, it provides the food that keep us alive for a longer period. Herbs, such as mint and sarsaparilla, can be planted in an 'ubi' and can be used to make healthy tea.

English:	Outdoors
Igbo:	Ezi
Breakdown:	'e' (partial positive) & 'zi'(teach, reveal, show)
Comments:	Ezi (outdoors) always have something to show or reveal to us. All we need to do is to pay attention to nature, and we will always learn something from the outdoors.

English:	Temple(Church)
Igbo:	Okwu
Breakdown:	'O' & 'kwu' (speak)
Comments:	Temple as a place where the Supreme being speaks or where men (or woman) speak about the Supreme being.

Chi, and healing words from an ancient language.

English:	Church
Igbo:	ụka
Breakdown:	'ụ' (prefix) & ' ka' (explain, talk or communicate)
Comments:	Church (or house of worship) as a place of talk or communication. A church provides a venue where members can communicate to each other about what God is doing in their lives. The verb 'ka' also means greater, because communication to God and man is greater than any other thing. Church activities put us in a more positive emotional state. Good emotional states are good for the Chi. The better our emotional state, the better our communication to God and man.

English:	Home
Igbo:	ụnọ
Breakdown:	'ụ' (community prefix used to intensify the power of a verb/noun) and 'nọ' (to be near another or together)
Comments:	Home is where people can be near one another or come together. The action a house communicates is togetherness. A house brings people together as a family.

English:	Way
Igbo:	ụzọ
Breakdown:	'ụ'(community Prefix) and 'zọ'(step) zọ is also 'save'. See nzoputa (salvation)
Comments:	A road (way) is a way to save lives, time, etc. ụzọ (dawn) is a way to save the day! One of the facts the Igbo is communicating, is that each time we take a step, we are actually creating roads. ụzọ = way=stepping. This is because our saved steps create roads. This is obvious when you see a path created on grass by steps.

Chi, and healing words from an ancient language.

In this image, walkers have created a 'road' in a golf course that recently closed down. Photo by Walter Baxter.

English:	Forest
Igbo:	ọffia
Breakdown:	'ọ' (prefix used for personal issues) & 'fia' (twisted, difficult)
Comments:	In the modern world, we may go to the forest to relax and be with nature, after we have carefully packed our food from Wholefoods or similar supermarkets. But a forest is an extremely difficult place to live in. To obtain food from a forest, we would need to hunt, and it is no easy task. Edible plants have to be sought, at the risk of snake and other animal bites. To live in the forest is to risk one's life. This is why the forest is considered twisted and difficult. When we have our own farms, things get much easier. The opposite of forest is market (affia).

Chi, and healing words from an ancient language.

Mathematics and Wealth

Numbers

English:	One, 1
Igbo:	Otu
Breakdown:	'O' (prefix) & 'tu' (oneness or togetherness)
Comments:	The number one represents wholeness or togetherness. For example, "we are one people". The verb **tu** is in the phrase 'kedụ ife ana e-**tu** gi? ' (what is your title?). Actually, the phrase means, 'what are you one with? In ancient times, people were 'one' with their title. If someone takes an eagle title, the purpose is to become 'one' with the eagle. This person is a stand for the eagle and acquires, the mannerisms of the eagle. The eagle is bold and confident.

English:	Two, 2
Igbo:	Abụa
Breakdown:	'a' (neutral prefix) & 'bụ'(being) & 'a' (neutral suffix)
Comments:	Knowledge of numbers and mathematics is important for understanding cultural and spiritual events. For example, a Traditional Igbo Person (TIP), does not accept gifts that are not in twos or multiples of twos. TIPs do not accept odd number gifts. They often cite the pairing of organs, as examples of how life presents itself in twos. In addition, it takes two to tango. A woman cannot conceive a child by herself. Two represents being or living.

Chi, and healing words from an ancient language.

English:	Three, 3
Igbo:	Atọ
Breakdown:	'a' (neutral prefix) & 'tọ'(to get stuck)
Comments:	The Igbos believe that numbers have spiritual implications. They believe that things get 'stuck' on the third time.

English:	Four, 4
Igbo:	Anọ
Breakdown:	'a'(neutral prefix) & 'nọ '(together, near another)
Comments:	A knowledge of numbers is useful in counting of days in the calendar. There are 4 days in the Igbo week called an 'Izu'. 'Izu' is from the verb 'zu' which is complete. Those four days are together. Four represents togetherness.

English:	Five, 5
Igbo:	Ise
Breakdown:	'I' (strongly positive prefix) & 'se' (separate)
Comments:	Each week has four days, and the fifth day 'separates' the weeks.

English:	Six
Igbo:	Isii
Breakdown:	'I' (strongly positive prefix) & 'sii'-further separation.
Comments:	The fifth is a separation of the 1st four. The sixth is a further separation.

English:	Seven
Igbo:	Isaa
Breakdown:	'I' (strongly positive prefix) & 'sa'-answer
Comments:	Seven has often been associated with God and Godly activities. God is there seeking communication, and always answers. Osa is a name for God.

English:	Eight
Igbo:	Isatọ, esatọ, asatọ
Breakdown:	'Ise' (five) & 'atọ' (three)
Comments:	8 = 5 + 3

English:	Nine
Igbo:	Itenani
Breakdown:	'Ite' (prolongation) & 'nani' (only)
Comments:	The number nine represents prolongation. The number ten is a more significant number.

English:	Ten
Igbo:	Iri
Breakdown:	'I' (strong positive prefix) & 'ri' (flow)
Comments:	It appears that they believe that when something reaches ten in number it begins to flow. This may be useful in a number of ways. For instance, a person might decide to 'eat' every 10th tuber of yam he possesses. The verb 'ri' is also seen in 'eating' because it is a way to 'flow' food. When an individual owns ten cars, watch and see if the 10th car will somehow 'flow' away. In the game of soccer, there are 10 players (and 1 goal keeper). The designers of the game understood that 10 players are need to create an optimum flow of the ball towards the opposite side. Not 7, 8, 9, 11, or 12 players. The number ten shirt is often worn by the best strikers. Pele, Maradona, and Ronaldo are examples.

Post Stamp; Edson Arantes do Nascimento (Pele)- one of soccer's greatest strikers.

Chi, and healing words from an ancient language.

Mathematics

English:	Add, addition
Igbo:	gbakọ
Breakdown:	'gba' (apply) & 'kọ' (ready)
Comments:	To add is to get something ready. Igbo is a practical language. Some of the uses of mathematics in Igbo include; 1. Recording and counting food-stock. 2. Counting money for the purposes of business, debt payment, and purchase of land and other property. 3. Social or religious purposes. A Traditional Igbo Person (TIP), only accepts even number gifts.

English:	Subtract
Igbo:	bere
Breakdown:	bere=to cut
Comments:	Subtraction is 'cutting' something from something.

English:	Fraction
Igbo:	Mpekele
Breakdown:	'Mpe' (small) & 'ke' (create) & 'le' (manifest)
Comments:	A fraction of something, is a manifestation of a smaller proportion.

English:	Portion or section.
Igbo:	Nke
Breakdown:	'n' (positive prefix) & 'ke' (creation)
Comments:	A portion is a creation.

Chi, and healing words from an ancient language.

English:	Half (division)
Igbo:	ọkara
Breakdown:	'ọ'(personal prefix) & 'ka' (greater) & 'ra' (leave)
Comments:	To divide something into half, is to ensure that none is greater.

English:	Week
Igbo:	Izu
Breakdown:	'I' (strongly positive prefix) & 'zu' (complete)
Comments:	Igbo uses a lunar calendar with 4 day weeks. Each week represents a completion of a lunar phase.

The significance of Igbo numbering system.

Knowledge of numbers is very important in any community. Yearly and seasonal festivals, and other important occasions demanded the accurate counting of days.

Kings, and their officials, needed these numbers to set dates, and plan for events. Stones may have been used to keep an accurate count of days.

Knowledge of numbers is also useful in keeping records of life-stock and food-stock. This is very important to the King and his officials. Kings often kept a reserve of food-stock and life-stock that could be useful in a drought or war. Accurate numbers, no doubt, would be helpful in decision making.

Furthermore, the average person needed to have a working knowledge of numbers, in order to participate in the weekly market activities.

The four market days eke, orie, afor, and nkwo are named after spirits that governed the days. Each day corresponds to one of the four cardinal points of the earth.

Chi, and healing words from an ancient language.

Market day	Cardinal point
Eke	East
Orie	West
Afọ	North
Nkwọ	South

In the lunar Igbo calendar, each week has 4 days and a total of 7 weeks makes one month. In other words, a month has 28 days. Incidentally, it takes the moon about 28 days to circle the earth.

Eke	Orie	Afọ	Nkwọ
		1	2
3	4	5	6
7	8	9	10
11	12	13	14
15	16	17	18
19	20	21	22
23	24	25	26
27	28		

This table is an example of an Igbo month.

Igbo villages often had one week day designated as a market day. On that day, people had the opportunity to exchange goods and services. We can readily deduce that understanding numbers would be helpful if one wanted to plan properly, and participate in the weekly market activities all year round.

The names of numbers were obtained from the experiences and social interactions, and from the practical and spiritual uses of that number. For example, the word for four 'anọ' was obtained from the verb 'nọ'. 'Nọ' is also seen in the word for house (ụnọ), and indicates togetherness. We can readily understand that every market day, which is every 4 days, is a time for togetherness.

Chi, and healing words from an ancient language.
It is important to note that Igbos must have participated in many ancient non-Igbo Kingdoms, and could have borrowed concepts and ideas from them.

This is a summary of the practical use of numbers.

Number	Igbo name	Meaning
1	Otu	The verb 'tu' indicates 'oneness'. It is seen in word for peer-group (otu), and in the word for title (tu).
2	abụa	The verb 'bụ' refers to 'being'. Things in life occur in twos. Organs of the body appear in twos. And life propagates in twos-male and female.
3	atọ	The verb tọ indicates to get stuck. It is believed that things get stuck on the third time.
4	anọ	This is from the verb 'nọ' which is togetherness. There are 4 days in the week, and every fourth day is a market day, that brings people together.
5	Ise	The verb 'se' indicates 'separation'. After the fourth item, the fifth is the beginning of a new lot.
6	Isii	Indicates a further separation.
7	Isaa	'sa' is the verb for answer. God is often associated with the number 7. Seven was frequently used in the old and new testaments of the Bible. God rested on the seventh day, the menorah has 7 lamps, and the wall of Jericho fell on the 7th day after seven priests blew 7 trumpets.
8	isatọ	Ise(5)+ atọ (3)=isatọ=8
9	Itenani	'Ite' is 'prolongation' and 'nani' is only. It appears that they couldn't readily find the symbolism for the use of the number 9. The 9th item apparently refers to 'prolongation only'.
10	Iri	The verb 'ri' indicates 'flow' and is found in the word for water (mmiri). Ten indicates a point of flow. Numbers after 10 indicate a

		different set of numbers compared to 1-10. Practically, an individual can set aside every 10th item for special use. For instance, an individual can set aside every 10th harvested yam for replanting the next season. In the Bible, every 10th of our possession was required as tithe to God (Genesis 14:18-20 Deuteronomy 14:23, Malachi 3:8-12).
11	Iri na otu	Ten plus one
12	Iri na abụa	Ten plus two
13	Iri na atọ	Ten plus three

Wealth

English:	Plenty, abundant
Igbo:	Rinne
Breakdown:	'Ri' (flow) & 'nne' (mother, source)
Comments:	Anything that is plenty or abundant is overflowing from its mother (source).

English:	Wealth
Igbo:	ụba
Breakdown:	'ụ' (prefix) & 'ba' (to enter, space for something to enter)
Comments:	Wealth is having increased capacity. See also Barn (Oba). To be wealthy is to be a reservoir. Wealthy people often have the ability to reach out to many people. They are directly or indirectly associated with large numbers of people. They make and/or receive large numbers of phone calls. To be wealthy, is to have a large capacity.

Chi, and healing words from an ancient language.

English:	Money
Igbo:	Ego
Breakdown:	'e' (prefix used as a partial positive) & 'go' (esteem)
Comments:	This is the same verb in ugo (eagle). We may never know what the first human forms of money was, but we know that having wealth can give us some self esteem.

English:	Debt
Igbo:	ụgwọ
Breakdown:	'ụ' (prefix) & 'gwọ' (to heal or make good)
Comments:	Debt is used to 'make good' or heal a lender. Do not lend someone unreliable money because it could cause you distress that can result to illness. That's why landlords feel 'sick' when they do not get their rent.

English:	Theft
Igbo:	Ori
Breakdown:	'O' (personal prefix) & 'ri' (to leak out, flow)
Comments:	In the modern world, people are imprisoned due to theft because of strong laws of ownership. Theft appears to be a phenomenon in which ones possessions "leak out" to other places. This perspective may help us deal with the painful emotion associated with loss of personal items.

English:	Market
Igbo:	Affia
Breakdown:	'a' (negative prefix) & 'fia' (twist, disorganize, difficult)
Comments:	This word illustrates an understanding of Marketing 101. Affia is the very opposite of forest which is called 'ọffia'. The verb 'fia' refers to twisting or disorganizing which represents a forest. One has to risk snake bites, animal predators, weak tree branches, e.tc. to obtain food from the forest. It is twisted and difficult. On the other hand, the items you are looking for have been 'untwisted' and organized in a market so it is quite easy to obtain. Marketing is, basically, untwisting items so it is easy for people to obtain it for their own use.

Chi, and healing words from an ancient language.

English:	Barn
Igbo:	ọba
Breakdown:	ọ (privative) 'ba' (from banye-enter)
Comments:	That which is a space for something. Space or reservoir

Physical objects

English:	Wall
Igbo:	Aja
Breakdown:	'a'(negative prefix) & 'ja' (rattle, communicate)
Comments:	In the modern world, we have erected an enormous amount of walls. This is obviously due to insecurity. Walls are erected in places we would not like to communicate with the outside world, such as bedrooms and living rooms. A wall indicates the opposite of communication. When a wall exists between two people one is forced to find other ways of communication.
	In the case of the Israelites, the people of Jericho did not want to communicate with them. The walls of Jericho was brought down by the sound of trumpets and by shouting (Joshua 6, 20).
	The verb 'ja' is also seen in the word for joke (njakiri).

Chi, and healing words from an ancient language.

Someone in this walled garden wouldn't readily want to communicate with the outside world. Image by Mike Smith.

English:	Stone- small stone
Igbo:	Iche
Breakdown:	'I' (strong positive prefix) & 'che' (wait, guard)
Comments:	Small stones were used to guard property in the past. Guards may hurl these stones at thieves, animals or invading armies. Slings were used to hurl stones in the past. Notice the similarity between guarding (nche) and stone (iche).

Chi, and healing words from an ancient language.

Small stones can be used to guard against birds, animals and even humans.

English:	Stone
Igbo:	Okwute
Breakdown:	'Okwu' (to speak) and 'te' (long)
Comments:	A stone as an instrument that can be used to make a statement over a prolonged period of time. When you build on stone, it offers you an opportunity to make a statement over countless generations. You can also cut messages into stone for posterity. Just like the ancient Egyptians did.

Chi, and healing words from an ancient language.

The ancient Egyptians made statements on stone that have lasted thousands of years. Image by Glenn Ashton.

English:	Stone, especially heavy stone.
Igbo:	Mkpume
Breakdown:	'Mkpu' (to mold) and 'ume' (strength)
Comments:	Heavy stone can be used for weight training. It can mold strength. Lie on a flat piece of rock and note how it molds your strength.

English:	Tools
Igbo:	Ngwọlụ
Breakdown:	'ngwọ' (healing, making good) and 'olụ' (work)
Comments:	Tools are used to do a good job. Or we use tools for 'making good' a work assignment. So it is important that we select the right tools we need to do a good job timely. A college degree can be considered a tool.

English:	Well (water well)
Igbo:	ụmi
Breakdown:	'ụ' (prefix used in community issues) and 'mi'(to suck, suction)
Comments:	A well functions like a straw. When we suck on a straw placed into a drink, we create an area of negative pressure in the throat that forces the water up. A well functions on the same principle. When you dig a narrow channel into the ground, you are creating an area of negative pressure that forces water up into the well. All you have to do is to dig close to the underground water table, and then leave the rest to the suction pressure. This word suggests that these ancient people knew basic engineering principles.

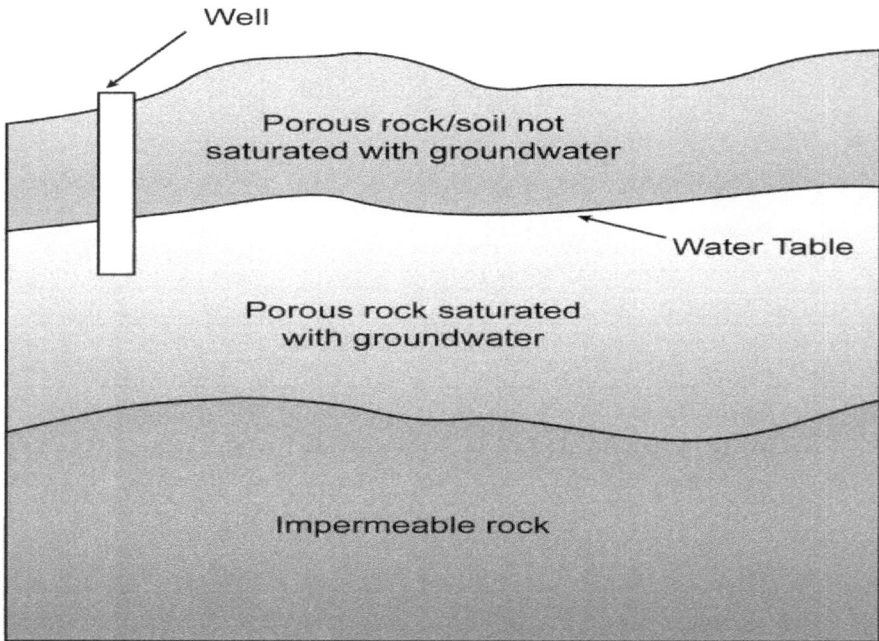

Water well description. Image by Geoff Ruth.

Chi, and healing words from an ancient language.

English:	Cup
Igbo:	Iko
Breakdown:	'I' (positive verb intensifier) & 'ko' (draw or scoop)
Comments:	The verb 'ko' is used in kolu (make a draw). Cups were used to draw water from a pot or similar vessels.

English:	Pot
Igbo:	Ite
Breakdown:	'I' (positive verb intensifier) & 'te' (prolong)
Comments:	The verb 'te' is also found in the word for mat 'ute'. Cooking prolongs our lives because it kills bacteria and other harmful organisms that might be in food. Cooking also helps extract nutrients from food. In addition, there are many nutritious food items that we may abandon because their taste isn't that great when raw. Co-incidentally, pots are usually made of fire resistant material and last for a very long time.

English:	Mat
Igbo:	Ute
Breakdown:	'U'(prefix used in multi-person or community to intensify a verb) & 'te' (long or prolong)
Comments:	Lie on a mat next to the earth and your life will be prolonged. When you lie on a mat next to the earth, the latter absorbs bad energy from your body. The word for "lie down" which is 'di nọ ana' in Igbo illustrates the point. 'Di nọ ana' actually is translated 'be with the earth' or 'be near the earth'. David also makes a similar point in Psalm 23 when he says; ".....he makes me lie down in green pastures, he restores my soul". When you lie on a mat next to the earth, the earth takes away your illnesses, gives you more strength and restores your soul.

Chi, and healing words from an ancient language.

English:	Chair
Igbo:	Oche.
Breakdown:	'O' (personal prefix) & 'che' (guard, wait)
Comments:	A chair is used to wait, and guards a person from falling to the ground.

English:	Cap, Hat
Igbo:	Okpu
Breakdown:	'O' (prefix used in personal issues) & 'kpu' (to cover)
Comments:	Cap or hat is a covering. The purpose of a hat is to cover the hair/head. It is a sign of humility and submission to God.

English:	Jewelry
Igbo:	ọna
Breakdown:	ọna (to go)
Comments:	Jewelry is temporary, it comes and goes. See ana (land, earth).

English:	Shoes
Igbo:	Akpụkpọụkwụ
Breakdown:	'a' (negative prefix) &'kpụ' (mold) & 'kpọ' (harden) & 'ụkwụ' (feet)
Comments:	Leather is made when the skin of animals is treated with special materials that causes hardening. Animal skin is soft and allows the animal to maneuver and function properly. Untreated, animal skin is more easily damaged by environmental forces. When it is treated and hardens (kpọ), it can then be used to make shoes.

Chi, and healing words from an ancient language.

English:	Rope
Igbo:	ụdọ
Breakdown:	'ụ' (community prefix) & 'dọ' (to restrain, or pull)
Comments:	Rope as restraint. The community prefix here suggests that the restraint is in the interest of the community. This is why animals are often tied with a rope or leash.

English:	Trap
Igbo:	ọnya
Breakdown:	'ọ' (prefix) & 'nya' (to carry or drive)
Comments:	A trap can seize an animal for you to carry away later.

English:	Arrow
Igbo:	ụta
Breakdown:	'ụ' (community prefix) & 'ta' (bite)
Comments:	The purpose of the bow and arrow is to 'bite' down animals or invading humans.

English:	Vehicle
Igbo:	ụgbọ
Breakdown:	'ụ' (community prefix) and 'gbọ' (to propel)
Comments:	'gbọ' is the verb used in vomiting because it is propulsion of stomach contents. A vehicle, whether it's used in water, land or air, is a propulsion system.

English:	Black(person or object)
Igbo:	Oji
Breakdown:	'O' (personal intensifier) and 'ji'(holder, reservoir, absorber)
Comments:	A black object or person absorbs light and is therefore a holder or absorber of light/energy. A black person as a holder of something. A black person always retains something.

Chi, and healing words from an ancient language.

English:	Poison
Igbo:	Nsi
Breakdown:	'N'(prefix) & 'si' (stop) N is an intensifier
Comments:	Poison as something that can stop a human, animal or other living things.

Physical motion and related concepts

English:	Start
Igbo:	bido
Breakdown:	'bi' (live) & 'do' (keep)
Comments:	One fundamental activity of living organisms is to 'start' something. A living being that cannot start anything might as well be considered dead. When we take a walk, we 'start' the foot somewhere and end it somewhere else.
	When we pick up a glass of water, we are 'starting' it from the table and ending near the mouth. So to start something is to 'keep living'.

English:	Wrestling
Igbo:	Mgba
Breakdown:	'm' (prefix) & 'gba' (apply)
Comments:	The aim of wresting is for opponents to try to 'apply' each other to the ground. Wrestling was and is still a major sport around the world. This sport tests many human attributes including raw strength and agility. When someone dies, there body is immobile and 'applied' to the ground. Burial is a form of permanent 'application' to the ground. We have all heard 'from dust we came and to dust we go'. The victor in a wrestling match is the person with the most ability to overcome death, and he proves this by 'applying' his opponent to the ground.

Chi, and healing words from an ancient language.

English:	Heavy
Igbo:	Nyi
Breakdown:	Nyi=beyond.
Comments:	A heavy object is something that is 'beyond' an individual. This individual cannot move it with ease, if at all.

English:	Heavy
Igbo:	Alụ
Breakdown:	'a' (negative prefix) & 'lụ' (work)
Comments:	A heavy object is something that is unworkable or not easily put to work. An individual who has a very heavy work tool, would not be able to work.

English:	Attach
Igbo:	Mgbado
Breakdown:	'mgba' (application) & 'do' (keep)
Comments:	Attachment is 'applied keeping'. To attach to someone is to keep something with someone. What is kept can be physical or mental. To detach, all we have to do is to find out what we have kept in the person, and retrieve it.

English:	Break
Igbo:	gbuji
Breakdown:	'gbu' (kill) & 'ji' (hold, bond)
Comments:	To break something is to kill the bond the holds it together.

English:	Leave
Igbo:	gbuji
Breakdown:	'gbu' (kill) & 'ji' (hold bond)
Comments:	To leave is to break or kill the bond that is holding you and the place you are in.

Chi, and healing words from an ancient language.

English:	Take
Igbo:	gụlụ
Breakdown:	gụlụ-is to make a count
Comments:	This word is often used when someone is asked to "take some meat from a pot". When we take something, we are inherently counting what we are taking. Taking necessitates counting or assessing what is being taken.

English:	wear
Igbo:	yi
Breakdown:	yi (resemble)
Comments:	When we wear clothing, we are actually trying to resemble (or look like) the clothing we are wearing. Clothing is an opportunity for us to send messages to the outside world about any theme we would like to communicate.

English:	Bring
Igbo:	Bute
Breakdown:	'bu' (carry) & 'te' (long, prolonged)
Comments:	To bring something is to carry it for a prolonged period.

English:	Slow, slowly
Igbo:	Nwayo
Breakdown:	'Nwa' (child) & 'yọ' (shake)
Comments:	This word captures the gentle motion that is used to soothe a child. When one does something slowly, one is approximating this gentle motion.

Chi, and healing words from an ancient language.

English:	Close
Igbo:	Kwuchi
Breakdown:	'Kwu' (speak) & 'chi' (end)
Comments:	This word also illustrates the consciousness of the ancient Igbos. They were not just in communication with living beings, they also communicated with non-living entities. For instance, a pot of soup can be considered to be 'speaking' when it is open. Its contents could be communicating something. When we close the pot, we are essentially 'ending the speech' from the pot. This applies to anything we close. It could be a house, a car, a mouth, or a container of body cream. ('Chi' is end from uzoechina or obiechina)

English:	Close
Igbo:	Mechi
Breakdown:	'me' (make) & 'chi' (end)
Comments:	See also kwuchi which as another variant of close. In mechi, when we close an object, we are essentially 'making an end' to the contents of the object. Whenever we close an object we are actually bringing an 'end' to whatever is in the object, albeit temporarily. Chi (end) is also found in the word for God (Chukwu, Chineke) because God is the beginning and the end (omega).

English:	Spoil, ruin
Igbo:	Mebie
Breakdown:	'me' (make) & 'bie' (end)
Comments:	To spoil something is to bring an end to it.

Chi, and healing words from an ancient language.

English:	High
Igbo:	Enu
Breakdown:	'e'(partial negative)& 'nu'(nudge, push)
Comments:	It is difficult to push objects or reach into a place that is high.

English:	Far
Igbo:	Teka
Breakdown:	'te' (prolonged) & 'ka' (greater)
Comments:	Two verbs are used in this case to yield far which is essentially 'greatly prolonged'.

Music and Musical instruments

English:	Talking Drum
Igbo:	Ekwe
Breakdown:	'e' (partial positive) & 'kwe' (agree)
Comments:	This musical instrument is used in ceremonies and events. It is also used as a 'talking drum' for communication. This drum can be used to communicate information between villages several miles apart. For the messages to be useful, there must be agreement as to what the sounds communicate.

Chi, and healing words from an ancient language.

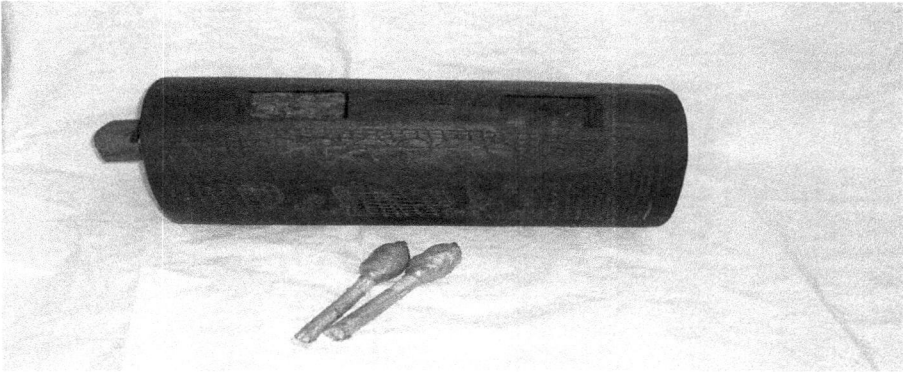

Ekwe

English:	Drum
Igbo:	Igba
Breakdown:	'I'(strong positive prefix) & 'gba' (apply)
Comments:	Although the modern successor of the drum is more commonly used in modern music, this ancient tool still retains its purpose to this day. The drum and its successors can be considered as a 'broad spectrum application system'. Drums used in music is intended to uplift members of the society emotionally so they can participate in what is going on. This is why drumming is an integral part of ceremonies, burials, and other events in African culture. Drumming helps create a favorable emotional state that brings people together. The same thing can be said about modern music as well. Concerts exploit this natural ability of drums to bring people together. It is not surprising that some musicians can attract thousands of people in one space.

Chi, and healing words from an ancient language.

Drummers performing at Marcus Garvey Park New York city.

English:	Gong
Igbo:	Ogene
Breakdown:	'O' (personal prefix) & 'ge' (time) and 'ene' (watch)
Comments:	The gong, a musical instrument, is used to draw the community to listen and watch on different occasions. Ogene is time to listen and watch.

Chi, and healing words from an ancient language.

Man playing a small gong in New York city.

English:	Horn (musical instrument)
Igbo:	Opi
Breakdown:	'O' (personal intensifier) and 'pi' (forward movement)
Comments:	This musical instrument (opi) is made from the horn (mpi) of animals such as rams, cattle, and elephants. They are used in religious and cultural ceremonies to announce processions and related events. Priests carrying ram horns were instrumental in bringing down the wall of Jericho. The verb 'pi' is in the word 'pia' (press forward).

Chi, and healing words from an ancient language.

Ram's horn. Walters Art Museum

Chi, and healing words from an ancient language.

English:	Flute
Igbo:	ọja
Breakdown:	'ọ' (personal intensifier) and 'ja' (rattle, communicate)
Comments:	This musical instrument is used to personally communicate with people during a musical performance. The flute can be used to send information analogous to spoken or sung words. It can be used solo or in combination with other musical instruments. Communication is a strong theme in Igbo music.

Solo performance with a flute.

Chi, and healing words from an ancient language.

The Body

English:	My body
Igbo:	arụ mụ
Breakdown:	'arụ' (body) & 'mụ' (my soul)
Comments:	I am not my body. It is just the covering of my soul. See also onwe mu(owner of my soul or my spirit).

English:	Lotion (body lotion)
Igbo:	Ude
Breakdown:	'U' (prefix used in community settings) & 'de' (straighten)
Comments:	The 'u' prefix suggests the skin has some value in the community. People enjoy looking at women with beautiful, smooth ('straightened out') skin. The skin is the largest organ in the body, and its health and beauty, is very important. Models with beautiful skin can demand higher fees. The verb 'de' is used in ironing clothing because it is a way to smoothen or straighten clothing.

English:	Head
Igbo:	Isi
Breakdown:	'I' (strong positive prefix) & 'si' (reinforce)
Comments:	The head is a reinforced structure. In most organisms, the head is very strong and 'armored'. This protects the brain of the organism and helps survive danger, especially after a predator attack. The head also contains other sense organs such as eyes, ears, and nose that helps an organism detect and escape, or subdue predators or prey. The verb 'si' is also used in the verb for cooking because cooking is 'reinforcing food'.

Chi, and healing words from an ancient language.

English:	Brain
Igbo:	ụbụru
Breakdown:	'ụ' (community prefix) & 'bụrụ' (being)
Comments:	The use of the 'ụ' prefix suggests the brain has a community orientation. The brain should be for community use. Our brain gives us our 'being'. Our 'being' determines what we are going to specialize in as a profession. A brain is only useful, if it is used to solve community problems, or provide service in a community.

English:	Eye
Igbo:	Anya
Breakdown:	'a' (negative) "nya" (it, as is). Anya is 'not it' or 'not as is'
Comments:	This is a powerful one. This word illustrates that the eye only creates mental image pictures. It is not the real thing or the complete picture. We should experience what we see with our other senses. Do not judge a book by its cover. Also do not be carried away, or be unduly influenced by what the eye sees. Using our eyes, we may judge the sun and the moon to be about the same distance from the earth. However, the sun is way, way farther away from the earth compared to the moon. Because the sound 'a' is also used in a neutral manner, the eye can also be assumed to produce images of reality, when it has been confirmed with the other senses.

English:	Mouth
Igbo:	ọnụ
Breakdown:	'ọ' (personal prefix) & 'nụ' (listen)
Comments:	That which creates that which you listen to. The mouth is also a listening tool. Sound actually reaches the inner ears through the teeth and jaw bones. Technology to listen to sound through the mouth has recently been developed to treat patients with conductive hearing loss. It is placed on the upper palate. The verb 'nụ' is also used to describe the act or ceremony

	in which a man marries a woman. Marriage is a listening or communication contract between two parties. When the communication is good, there is more love.

English:	Teeth
Igbo:	Eze
Breakdown:	'e'(partial positive) & 'ze'(guard, protect)
Comments:	Eze (teeth) is slightly phonetically different from Eze (king) But they convey the same action-protection or guarding. When you holistically examine the function of teeth, in a gamut of organisms, you would readily note that it is a protective organ. It can be readily used for defense or attack. In humans and in some animals, biting often accompanies love making (love bites). So the teeth is somewhat a symbol of love. This ties in with the word of God from 1 Corinthians Chapter 13 vs 7 that 'love always protects'. Many Igbo masquerades also feature oversized teeth. This is because teeth represents protection and love.

English:	Tongue
Igbo:	Ile
Breakdown:	'I' (positive prefix) and 'le' (manifest)
Comments:	We all know there is power in the spoken word, and we are all familiar with the phrase "watch your tongue". What we say plays a strong role in creating our universe.

English:	Neck
Igbo:	Onu
Breakdown:	'O' & 'nu' (push) is also voice
Comments:	The voice box in the neck is a very important structure. Without it we would not be able to develop language, and co-coordinating multiple community issues would be difficult. The voice allows us to push the matters that concern us to resolution.

Chi, and healing words from an ancient language.

English:	Arm pit
Igbo:	Mkpabu
Breakdown:	'mkpa' (scatter) & 'bu' (being)
Comments:	The armpit is the main source of body odor, and every individual has a unique odor. Body odor is known to play a role in sexual selection. Mothers can distinguish their offspring from others based on their body odor. People have unique sets of chemicals that determine body odor.

English:	Hand, Help
Igbo:	Aka
Breakdown:	'a' (negative prefix) & 'ka'(greater)= 'not greater'.
Comments:	The word for help is the same as the one for hand because our hand is our help. The hand is over represented in the brain, and this illustrates its importance. Without our hands, we are disabled. Although we use our hands to fashion a desirable physical universe, the hands receives instruction from higher centers such as the spirit and the mind. This is why the hands are 'not greater'. They are 'not greater than the mind or spirit.

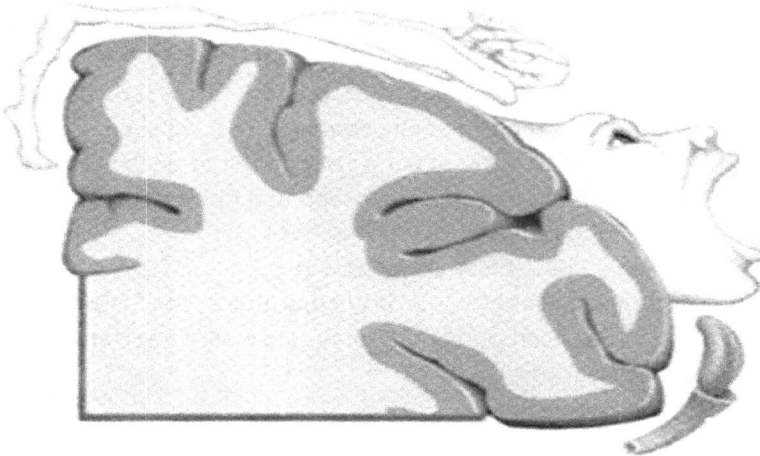

Motor homunculus of the brain showing the disproportionate representation of the hands.

Chi, and healing words from an ancient language.

English:	Breast
Igbo:	Ala
Breakdown:	"A"(neutral prefix) and "la"(to lick)
Comments:	Ala (breast) is derived from the verb 'la' (to lick). Basically, the breast is 'commanding' to be licked by a baby or a lover. Breast feeding helps prevent numerous illnesses, and has numerous advantages. It is the best food for a newborn and promotes maternal bonding.

English:	Heart
Igbo:	Obi
Breakdown:	'O' & 'bi' (to live, to be alive) O is an intensifier used in personal terms.
Comments:	That which makes you live. One dies when the heart stops. This demonstrates a practical Igbo understanding of anatomy and physiology.

English:	Belly
Igbo:	Afọ
Breakdown:	'a' & 'fọ' (remain) 'a' creates the negative
Comments:	Big belly as that which causes early death or that which prevents you from remaining standing. This word is warning us of the dangers of a poor diet, and that the development of a pot belly can lead to a number of medical conditions. Abdominal obesity is associated with hypertension/diabetes/obesity/Syndrome X/cancer and other medical conditions that may cause early mortality. See also ọffọr (ọfọ).

Chi, and healing words from an ancient language.

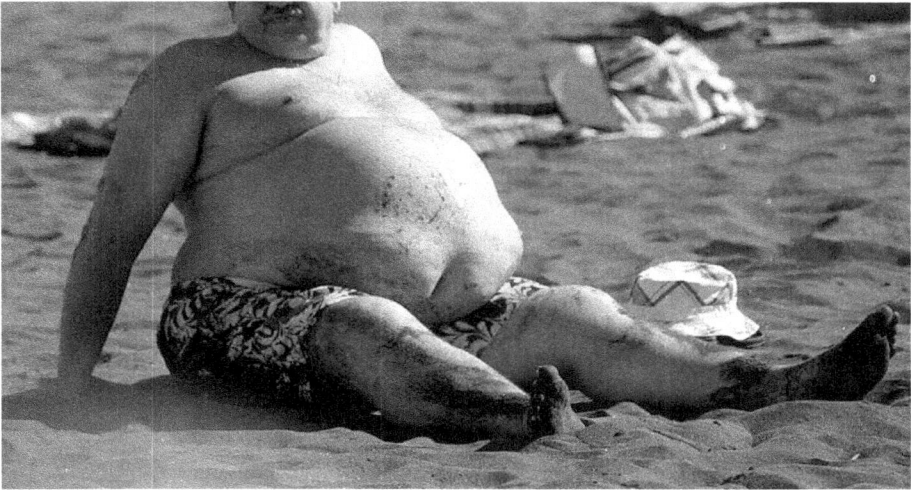

Abdominal obesity increases the risk of death. Image by Tibor Vegh.

English:	Intestines
Igbo:	Mgbiligb-afọ
Breakdown:	'mgbiligba' (bell) & 'afọ' (belly)
Comments:	The intestines are considered to function as the bells of the belly. The intestines can make noises when we are hungry, or when we eat foods that are not good for us. For example, patients that have milk intolerance can have 'rumblings' when they drink milk that suggests they should see their doctor.

English:	Liver
Igbo:	Umeju
Breakdown:	'ume' (energy) and 'ju' (full)
Comments:	Energy store house-biochemically the liver is an energy storehouse. This illustrates an Igbo understanding of the role of the liver in the body.

Chi, and healing words from an ancient language.

English:	Kidney
Igbo:	Akụ
Breakdown:	'a'(negative prefix) & 'kụ'(to knock or break down)
Comments:	That which prevents the body from breaking down. The kidney plays critical metabolic and hormonal roles that prevents the body from breaking down.

English:	Vagina
Igbo:	ọtụ
Breakdown:	'ọ' (prefix) & 'tụ' (to charm, draw or magnetize) Here ọ is a prefix used for personal issues.
Comments:	The vagina is very charming, and one can get magnetized. There are natural ways to increase the charm of the vagina. Shaving, trimming, or styling vaginal hair may be a good start.

English:	Penis
Igbo:	Amụ
Breakdown:	'a' (negative prefix) & 'mụ'(to learn)
Comments:	The penis is unlearned. This semen-spitting organ can do the same thing over and over again for a lifetime. It never gets satisfied, neither does it advance into a higher 'class'. This could explain why men in powerful positions risk their careers and family just to have sex. A wise individual exerts his mind and spirit over the penis which can be considered the 'Achilles heel' of men.

English:	Urine
Igbo:	Amiri
Breakdown:	'a' (negative prefix) & 'miri' (water)
Comments:	Urine is produced after water has been extracted from waste material in the kidneys. Basically, urine is suggesting 'without water'.

Chi, and healing words from an ancient language.

English:	Bone
Igbo:	ọkpụkpụ
Breakdown:	'ọ'(prefix) & 'kpụ' (mold) & 'kpụ' (mold)
Comments:	Bone as the mold in which the body is molded from.

English:	Knee
Igbo:	Ikpele
Breakdown:	'I'(prefix) & 'kpe' (report, confess, reveal) & 'le'(manifest, actualize)
Comments:	The knee appears to be an important spiritual tool for prayer (ekpele). They are most probably derived from the same words and the two should go hand in hand. "I" is an intensifier, it appears that when one performs a prayer with the knees to the ground, the power of the prayer is intensified. Basically, after prayer, the knee is what is used to carry the body to a location where the prayer is actualized. The knee is a major weight bearing joint in the body, and free movement is not possible without a healthy knee.

English:	Leg
Igbo:	ụkwụ
Breakdown:	'ụ' (prefix) & 'kwụ' (stand)
Comments:	That which is used to remain standing.

English:	Foot
Igbo:	ọkpa
Breakdown:	'ọ' (personal prefix) & 'kpa' (to scatter, shuffle)—see stars (kpakpando)
Comments:	Used for animals-that which is used to shuffle the earth.

Chi, and healing words from an ancient language.

English:	Feces
Igbo:	Nsi
Breakdown:	'N'& 'si' (stop) N is an intensifier
Comments:	Feces as poison. Contains bacteria and other micro-organisms that can cause ill health. The smell of feces is also a 'stopper' in the sense that it can prevent someone from coming closer.

Selected Diseases

English:	Illness
Igbo:	arụ na anwụ mụ
Breakdown:	'arụ' (body) & 'na' (is)& a 'nwụ' (die) & 'mụ' (my soul)
Comments:	In a spiritual society, humans are not their bodies. A physical illness is a condition in which a dysfunction of the body is causing death to the soul. The soul connects the spirit to the body. The soul recovers with the treatment of the physical illness.

English:	Malaise (general aches and pains)
Igbo:	arụ na egbụ mụ
Breakdown:	'arụ' (body)& 'na' (is) 'egbụ' (killing) & 'mụ' (my soul)
Comments:	In this condition, pain is killing the soul. The soul is used in learning and computing every day problems. Pain affects the quality of our mind. People in pain, view life differently and can be dangerous.

English:	Diarrhea, running stomach
Igbo:	Afọ-ọsisa
Breakdown:	'afọ' (abdomen, belly) & 'ọsisa' (washing)
Comments:	Diarrhea can be a life threatening condition and in developing countries, it's a major cause of infant mortality. The main stay of the management of this condition is fluid replacement. This condition can be considered as 'washing belly', and since you need water

> to do any type of washing, one has to introduce adequate fluids into the gastro-intestinal tract when this disease arises. An understanding of this concept would help mothers readily reach for fluids, once their children develop diarrhea.

English:	Malaria
Igbo:	Iba
Breakdown:	'I' (strong prefix) & 'ba' (enter)
Comments:	When a Mosquito 'enters' this parasite inside of an individual, the victim has 'entered'. They would not be able to enjoy life in the outside world like others. They need to be nursed inside the house or in a health care facility. In addition, the disease creates central nervous system side effects that literally takes patients to another world. Cerebral malaria leads to coma.

English:	Vomitus
Igbo:	Agbọ
Breakdown:	'a' (negative prefix) & 'gbọ' (propel, project)
Comments:	The verb 'gbọ' is also seen in 'ugbọ'(vehicle). The contents of the stomach and small intestines are not intended to be projected out of the body. Normally, intestinal contents are propelled, in the opposite direction, towards the anus. Vomiting is only useful in rare medical conditions such as the recent ingestion of a non-corrosive poisonous substance. Vomiting 'igbọ agbọ' actually means propelling the 'unpropelled'.

English:	Swelling (of body)
Igbo:	Akpu
Breakdown:	'a' (negative prefix) and 'kpu' (mold)
Comments:	Kpu is something molded and strong. The use of 'a' creates the opposite word. Soft tissue swellings of the body often respond to treatment fairly rapidly. A slight phonological variation differentiates this from the cassava meal.

Chi, and healing words from an ancient language.

English:	Scabies or similar skin conditions
Igbo:	Akpụkpa
Breakdown:	'akpụ' (swelling) and 'kpa' (scattered)
Comments:	Scabies is caused by the mite Sarcoptes scabiei. It is characterized by a rash that is commonly seen in the feet, buttocks, genitals, back, hands, wrists, and elbows. This is why it is called 'scattered swelling'.

English:	Psychosis, madness
Igbo:	Mgbaka- Isi
Breakdown:	'mgba' (application) & 'ka' (greater) &'isi' (head)
Comments:	Humans comprise a body, a mind, and spirit. In ideal (normal) circumstances, the spirit controls the mind, while the mind exerts control over the body. In psychosis, the 'head' takes great pre-eminence over the spirit and results in the signs and symptoms of this disease. In this condition, the spirit (thinking stuff) has lost control of the individual.

English:	Stress
Igbo:	mgbaka-arụ
Breakdown:	'mgba' (application) & 'ka' (greater) & 'arụ' (body)
Comments:	Normally, the spirit exerts control over the mind which in turn exerts control over the body. However, in this condition, the body is disproportionately in charge of the individual. The body does not possess pure 'thinking stuff' which the spirit has. This explains why stressed people have poor work results. They do not fare well in relationships either.

Chi, and healing words from an ancient language.

The use of breath in healing.

English:	Lungs
Igbo:	Ngụgụ
Breakdown:	'n' (positive prefix) and 'gụgụ' (heal or console)
Comments:	We can use our lungs to console or heal ourselves. There is scientific evidence that when we slow our breath to about 3-6 cycles per minute, after 10 minutes, we begin to feel a sense of well-being. This is useful for stress, anxiety, depression, worry, post-traumatic stress disorder, phobias, pain, and respiratory problems. This breathing pattern is very helpful for insomnia.

English:	Breath
Igbo:	Ume
Breakdown:	'U' (prefix) & 'me' (to do, make)
Comments:	Obviously, to be able to do anything we need to breath. Death is characterized by inability to breath.

English:	Strength or energy.
Igbo:	Ume
Breakdown:	'u'(prefix used in community settings) and 'me'(to do, make)
Comments:	Strength is required to do stuff or make thing happen. The Igbos use the same word for breath and energy because they are essentially the same concept. When we have shallow breath, we tend to have less energy. When we breath slow and deep, our energy increases. We can state that breath is intimately related to our energy levels.

Chi, and healing words from an ancient language.

English:	Behavior
Igbo:	Ume
Breakdown:	'U' (prefix) & 'me' (to do, make, action)
Comments:	It is easy to observe that our actions illustrate our behavior. Although this word is slightly phonologically different from the Ume (breath, or energy) they have the same verb. This is because our breathing pattern affects our energy levels, which in turn has an impact on our actions. People whose behavioral patterns include fear and anxiety tend to have a different breathing pattern compared to those that are calm and confident.

English:	Calm breath
Igbo:	Umeana
Breakdown:	'Ume' (breath) & 'ana' (earth)
Comments:	Our breathing pattern affects our behavior. People who have a calm breath can be meticulous in their action(s). To achieve this state, one has to draw slow deep breaths to the extent that, metaphorically, the inhalation reaches the earth through the abdomen and legs. They can also practice slow deep breaths while lying on the earth (floor).

English:	Coherent breath
Igbo:	Ude
Breakdown:	'U' (community prefix) & 'de' (straighten, smoothen)
Comments:	'Ude' is commonly observed in the elderly and children with severe malaria. It is characterized by a slow and deep inspiration, and an audible expiration. It is similar to the ujjayi breath or coherent breathing seen in yoga and other eastern breath practices. 'Ude' is a way to check the excess activity of the sympathetic (stress response) system. It up-regulates the opposing parasympathetic system. The sympathetic nervous system is responsible for secreting adrenalin and corticosteroids in preparation for 'flight or fight'. Chronic stimulation of the sympathetic

Chi, and healing words from an ancient language.

> nervous system, by stress or illness, is harmful to the
> body. Ude induces wellness by increasing the activity of
> the opposing parasympathetic nervous system.

Breath work in Igbo culture

Linguistics provides us with the opportunity of exploring the Igbo understanding of the role of breath in healing.

Igbos use the same word 'ume' for breath and energy. This indicates an understanding of the close relationship between the two concepts. A closely related (but phonologically different) word 'ume' indicates behavior. This is a clear statement of the inter-relatedness of these subjects.

The relationship between breath, energy and behavior is well known in Yoga, Tai Chi, and other cultural healing methods around the world.

Furthermore, the language describes a breathing pattern similar to the ocean breath of yoga as 'ude'. 'Ude' is commonly observed in children and old individuals suffering from Malaria. Scientific studies suggest that this breathing pattern has a healing effect, by up-regulating the parasympathetic nervous system.

Finally, the word for lungs 'ngụgụ' was coined from gụgụ which means to heal or console. When we slow our breaths to approximately 3-6 breaths a minute, after about 10 minutes, we begin to have a sense of well being.

   It is well known that anger, stress, anxiety and other negative emotions can induce disease in organs of the body such as the gastro-intestinal tract.

Impulses from the diseased organs are carried via the vagus nerves to the interoceptive cortex where they are registered in the higher centers.

The interoceptive cortex handles sensation from the internal organs, while the somatosensory cortex handles sensations that originate outside the body. The lung alveoli are rich in vagus nerve endings. When we slow and deepen our breaths to about 3-6 cycles per minute, more of those nerves are activated. The impulses are carried via the vagus to the interoceptive cortex from where

Chi, and healing words from an ancient language.
they are processed by the higher centers as subjective sensation of 'well being'. This helps explain how healing breath can make us feel much better.

Basically, healing breath helps counteract the effects of other negative emotions. When our Chi (personal guardian) contains more positive than negative emotions, we tend to have more success than failures.

The Mind

English:	Thought(good thought), wisdom
Igbo:	Uche
Breakdown:	'u' (prefix) & 'che' (wait or guard)
Comments:	Thought is actually meditation by waiting. To think is to wait.

English:	Postulate
Igbo:	Elo
Breakdown:	'e' (prefix used as a partial negative) and 'lo' (to throw out a thought)
Comments:	Postulation appears to come directly from the human spirit. It is a higher form of thought compared to what the mind originates. The spirit constantly makes assessments of its condition, and using information from the mind, makes postulates on how to improve our lives. This is why it is good to be in a good spiritual state so one can perform activities that are good for oneself. The state of the Chi is very important. When the Chi contains love, joy, happiness and other positive emotions, the mind correctly interprets and processes postulates. However, when anger, sadness and other negative emotions are present, the ability of the mind to correctly process postulates is hindered.

Chi, and healing words from an ancient language.

English:	Life
Igbo:	Ndu
Breakdown:	'N' (positive prefix) & 'du' (is, to be)
Comments:	Life is just 'to be'. It is just 'being'. Every life form is unique in that they have their own unique being. That unique being allows them to act in a certain way to attract more life to them. Basically how we are (our being) determines the type of actions we take and this in turn determines what we are going to have.

English:	Joke
Igbo:	Njakiri
Breakdown:	'n'(prefix) & 'ja' (communicate, rattle) & 'kiri' (small)
Comments:	A joke is 'small communication' or 'small rattling'. A joke is an indirect way to communicate a message. Jokes are useful when direct complete communication of a subject may lead to negative emotions. Jokes have social value because they communicate ideas without making others feel very bad. This can explain why comedians can be quite successful in the modern world.

English:	Yours (your portion)
Igbo:	Nke-gi
Breakdown:	'n'(positive prefix) & 'ke'(creation) & gi (you)
Comments:	Anything that belongs to you is your creation. You may own a smart phone with sophisticated technology, and this may be hard to believe. Yet, if you paid for it, and it belongs to you, then it is your creation.

English:	Sleep
Igbo:	ụla
Breakdown:	U (prefix used in community or multi-person occasions to enhance the power of a verb/noun and "la" (go away)
Comments:	Sleep as a way of' going away' to rest the brain and body. We should ensure we are getting adequate sleep. It is a 'holiday' we get every day, we often take for granted.

Chi, and healing words from an ancient language.

English:	Dream
Igbo:	Nlọ
Breakdown:	n(positive prefix) & 'lọ' (indirect)
Comments:	The verb 'lọ' is seen in 'eyeing'(ilọ anya). Eyeing someone is an indirect way of viewing the person. The verb is also seen in 'lọgọ' which means to 'twist' or 'make indirect'. A dream is an indirect way of viewing life phenomenon. People who understand this phenomenon, and who grasp the angle in which the dream occurred, can interpret dreams. The Biblical Joseph had the gift of interpretation of dreams. People can also receive indirect messages in dreams.

English:	Accuse, blame
Igbo:	ụta
Breakdown:	'ụ' (community prefix) & 'ta' (bite)
Comments:	To accuse someone is a way to spiritually or emotionally bite them.

English:	Progress
Igbo:	ọganiru
Breakdown:	'ọga' (to go) 'na' (in) & 'iru' (in front)
Comments:	'na' is used as a conjunction to marry the phrases 'to go' and 'in front'. Progress is being in the forefront of any activity or endeavor. If a community is seeking good health for all, they need to be at the forefront of health care delivery. The same applies to individuals seeking progress in any areas of their life.

Chi, and healing words from an ancient language.

English:	Faith
Igbo:	Okwukwe
Breakdown:	'okwu' (word) & 'kwe' (agree)
Comments:	To have faith is to agree with the word of God. Agree with God's word and it will be well with you. In all religions, we notice that God has kind words for us. He has plans for us even when we remain sinners. God is saying, " I know you sinned and come short of my glory, but let Me worry for you". All we have to do is to agree with His word to have a good life.

English:	Behavior
Igbo:	Omume
Breakdown:	'o' (personal prefix) & 'mụ' (me) & 'me'(maker, doer)
Comments:	Behavior; I am the doer/maker. Each individual should take responsibility for their behavior, as an individual's behavior, is a personal creation. We have to ensure that our behavior is consistent with the life we are trying to create. Knowledge of the Chi is very important if we desire to behave well. Negative emotions must be continually uprooted from the Chi.

English:	Attempt, Try
Igbo:	Sika
Breakdown:	'si' (stop) & 'ka' (greater)
Comments:	This 'si' is phonologically slightly different from the one in stubbornness and cooking. An attempt is greater than doing nothing. We are encouraged to attempt good stuff.

Chi, and healing words from an ancient language.

English:	Contribution
Igbo:	ụtụ
Breakdown:	'ụtụ' (charm or hook) see also vagina (ọtụ)
Comments:	Contribution is a process in which people are sold an inspiring activity, in a manner that compels them to throw in their support, in the form of money or similar resources.

English:	Voice
Igbo:	Onu
Breakdown:	'O' & 'nu' (push)
Comments:	Voice of a people creates language or words that can push issues that are a concern for that group. See also enu (sky).

English:	Shout, shouting
Igbo:	Mkpu
Breakdown:	'm' (prefix)& 'kpu' (cover)
Comments:	Shouting is used to 'cover' or 'drown' other voices (or sounds) so you can be heard, especially in a time of danger.

English:	Fight
Igbo:	ọgụ
Breakdown:	'ọ' (personal intensifier) and 'gụ' (hunger)
Comments:	We are all familiar with the phrase a 'hungry man is an angry man'. A 'hunger' for some person or item always precipitates a fight. Whenever there is a fight, always look for the precipitating cause, which sometimes is not visible to the fighting parties.

Chi, and healing words from an ancient language.

The Emotions

Negative emotions

English:	Oppression
Igbo:	Mmegbu
Breakdown:	'Mme' (action) & 'gbu' (kill)= killing.
Comments:	The feeling of oppression is one of the worst emotions. When people are oppressed, their spirit is being killed. They cannot express themselves, and are a slave to others. Every day, people are oppressed in their countries, in work places, and in relationships. My advice is to get away, and stay away, from an oppressive environment (or person), as soon as possible. Oppression is very bad for the Chi.

English:	Suffering
Igbo:	Afụfụ
Breakdown:	'a' (negative prefix) and 'fụ'(painful) and 'fụ' (painful)
Comments:	Suffering as a state characterized as painless painfulness. Suffering is all in the mind. Suffering will yield joy, happiness and painlessness later!

English:	Jealousy
Igbo:	Anyaufu
Breakdown:	'anya' (eye, view) & 'ufu' (pain, painful)
Comments:	Igbos appear to be quite good at Psychology. Jealousy is One of the negative emotions while love and happiness are positive emotions. They understood that jealousy is an emotion that is activated by pain. A jealous individual usually has preexisting pain, and his/her views are colored by this pain. This is what brings about jealousy. Jealousy is easily provoked, when the person the jealousy is directed at, caused someone pain earlier on. When we feel jealous, we should self examine for preexisting pain, and find ways to remove it. Jealousy has a negative impact on the Chi.

English:	Quarrel (quarrelling)
Igbo:	Ise-okwu
Breakdown:	'I' (strong positive prefix) & 'se' (separate) & 'okwu' (speech)
Comments:	We have all noticed people quarrelling. Countries even quarrel to the point of war. People even fight and die, because of quarrels. However, the underlying problem in quarrelling does not require blood-shed. Quarrelling is just a separation of 'words'. There is disagreement with the words each party is producing. Resolving a conflict may require an analysis of the words each party is producing in order to find common ground.

English:	Stubborness
Igbo:	Isi - ọnwụ
Breakdown:	'I' (strong positive prefix) & 'si' (reinforce, cook) & ọnwụ (death)
Comments:	Stubbornness is, generally, not accepted as a good attribute for anyone. It is not recognized as a positive state of being. A stubborn person is inviting his own physical or spiritual death. One of the ways to fight stubbornness may be to engage in physical activity such as playing a sport or dancing.

English:	Anger
Igbo:	Iwe
Breakdown:	'I' (verb intensifier) & 'we' (withdrawal)
Comments:	Anger is one of the negative emotions. More positive emotions include love and joy. Those who are in good emotional states have good quality thoughts. Individuals who are in poor emotional states, such as anger, have their thought quality hampered. An angry person is basically withdrawn. It is very difficult to talk or communicate with such a person. When an angry person acts, it is usually quite thoughtless and destructive. This is because their true self has 'withdrawn', and what is left is wreaking the havoc. It is important to avoid anger and angry people as much as possible. One sure way to have misfortune is to have a Chi that is drenched with anger.

Chi, and healing words from an ancient language.

English:	Boasting, aggrandizement, Self praise
Igbo:	Itu- ọnụ
Breakdown:	'I' (verb intensifier) & 'tu' (oneness) & 'ọnụ' (mouth) . See also One(1) 'otu'.
Comments:	When people practice self aggrandizement they unknowingly belittle themselves. While a human being comprises a spirit soul and body, a person who engages in self-praise is only becoming one with his/her mouth. In this unusual condition, the centers that govern the mouth in the brain have gained pre-eminence and is directing the persons being.

English:	Shy, Shyness
Igbo:	Ifele
Breakdown:	'Ife' (something) & 'e' (partial negative) & 'le' (manifest)
Comments:	Shyness is a negative emotion that can prevent us from manifesting our heart desires and objectives.

Mbọ -revenge

Mbọlu-making revenge.

Revenge is a very important subject in every culture and spirituality. If we look at revenge in Christianity, we note that a certain action is prescribed. Moses had recommended an eye for an eye (tit for tat). This action must have been examined, and upheld, by many prophets that followed Moses like Jeremiah, Nehemiah, Elijah, and even John the Baptist. To the dismay of his fellow Hebrews, Jesus overturned the law and recommended 'turn the other cheek'. The action Jesus had recommended for revenge, was the very opposite of 'tit for tat'. Jesus wanted us to show love to our enemies.

But how did the ancient Igbo's consider revenge? What action did they prescribe as revenge? How should we revenge? The answer to that question

Chi, and healing words from an ancient language.
lies in the Igbo word for revenge 'mbọ'. Igbo as we know, is a verb based language. The word mbọ contains a verb or action word that denotes revenge.

Before we go into that verb or action word, I would like us to consider two closely related words. These words are closely related morphologically, semantically, and phonetically but are words for different subjects.

The first is 'mbọ'; which is the word for nail(s).

The second is 'mbọ' which is the word for hard or effective work.

So what do nails, effective work and revenge have in common?

How could these three entirely different subjects share a common motion or action?

To understand ancient Igbo; I would like to tell you a short story. You can call it a parable if you choose.

"In ancient times the Igbo were primarily an agricultural society; most people were farmers.

On one cool but sunny day, a prominent spiritual man was recalled to his house due to an emergency. As he approached his house, he noticed a small silent crowd. He was beckoned towards his house. As he entered, he heard moans and groans emanating from his bedroom. He walked closer and as he opened the door he noticed a trusted friend on top of his wife.

Being spiritual and strong, he had a larger than normal hoe which he brought with him from the farm.

His grip hardened as rage diverted blood away from the centers of the brain that governed reasoning.

But from his spirit he heard the Igbo word for revenge; mbọ, mbọ, mbọ.

So he stepped back, turned around, and walked increasingly faster out of the house and towards the farm, then he broke into a sprint. When he got into the farm, he dug, dug, dug, and dug. He enriched mounds, made new ones,

Chi, and healing words from an ancient language. and removed weeds. When he finished, the Sun was setting and when he looked at his farm it was very beautiful. It was as if he had made a new hair style on mother earth, and mother earth was smiling.

When he got back home, his house was empty. He was soon joined by a young lady who was very impressed by his action, and asked him why he did not kill the man, adding that "everyone would understand". The Nze (a shepherd priest) replied, "there is nothing to be impressed about". What I have done, today, has been repeatedly performed by men before me. He brought some palm wine out, and served the lady. "Chinyere (her name)" he said; "notice that I am not cleaning up blood, and I would not be facing the elders to determine if my actions are justified or not". "you see, our word for revenge mbọ is derived from bọ which is the verb to dig". "We revenge by going back to work to dig, and dig deeper. "That is the ultimate revenge", he said".

The verb bọ is used in the word for nail (mbọ) because the nail is used for digging (animals), or women use it to dig into the skin of their lovers. 'Bọ' is also the action word for hard work (mbo) because in an agricultural society the only way to work hard and effective is dig, dig, dig (deeper). Dig out the weeds that compete with your crops for nutrients. Weeds are barriers to success.

In Igbo, the prescribed action for revenge (mbọ) is to dig deeper into your work, digging out the barriers (weeds) to success; whether you are a farmer, doctor, lawyer, nurse or a shoe maker.

The goals of a human being in a good mental condition should not include revenge against any group or person.

Revenge ravages the Chi because it is coupled with other negative emotions. In the above case, feelings or revenge would be accompanied by emotions of disbelief, anger, shock, distrust and a host of other negative emotions he must have experienced when he caught his wife cheating.

To be walking around with the emotions of revenge, is like taking your car for a service, but instead of ordering high grade motor oil, you ask for sand to be poured into the engine of your automobile.

Chi, and healing words from an ancient language.

Adolf Hitler is a perfect example of how revenge can wreak indescribable damage. The opposite of revenge is forgiveness. Forgiveness is no easy task, and requires mental homework. See forgiveness technology.

Once forgiveness is achieved, we can go back to our work and keep digging.

Adolf Hitler, and the danger of hate and revenge. Image by German federal archives.

English:	Pride
Igbo:	Ngala
Breakdown:	'Nga' (place) & 'la' (going away)
Comments:	Some say 'pride comes before the fall', and Igbo seems to agree. Pride is a 'place' one gets to, then starts 'going away'. Some individuals start their careers humble, and begin to record successes. Subsequently, this emotion creeps in, and leads to their fall. Adolf Hitler and Saddam Hussein are examples of how pride can lead to the demise of individuals, and cause incredible destruction.

Chi, and healing words from an ancient language.

English:	Fear
Igbo:	Egwu
Breakdown:	'e' (prefix used as a partial negative) & 'gwu' (to play, to game)
Comments:	Fear is a negative emotion. It has a deleterious effect on the Chi. Fear prevents us from participating fully in the game of life. Individuals with phobias, can be highly restricted. If we want our Chi to be in the optimum condition, we have to find effective ways to deal with our fears.

Positive emotions

Sacrifice in Ancient Igbo

Sacrifice is an important component of spirituality. Compared to Abraham whom God advised to sacrifice his son Isaac, we have it much easier. In modern times, we are often only required to sacrifice some part of our income in terms of money.

People sacrifice huge sums of money to support the lavish lifestyles of some Pastors. Some are reported to own chauffeured Rolled Royce and private jets.

The only explanation is that sacrifice works for givers.

But why does it work?

The answer is in the ancient Igbo word for sacrifice 'ichụ-aja'.

This word illustrates the degree of sophistication of the extra-terrestrials that created Igbo (language).

Chi, and healing words from an ancient language.

'Ichụ' denotes to 'chase away' and 'aja' is from the verb 'ja' which is to 'communicate'. The sound 'a' is used to reverse the notion of communication making 'aja'-lack of communication.

Simply, ichụ-aja is chasing away 'lack of communication'.

In other words, sacrifice (ichụ-aja) is 'enhancing communication'.

Sacrifice enhances our communication with God that leads to His answers to everyday challenges.

Sacrifice gives us an unprecedented ability to communicate with church leaders, church members and people in general.

The more you sacrifice (or give) the more you chase away negative communication.

Because an 'enhanced communication' is a state of being, which we can carry to our work places and businesses; it results in success with money.

So don't expect the private jets to be grounded soon.

Sacrifice and walls

The 'aja' in sacrifice carries the same theme as the phonetically similar 'aja' (wall). A wall is a barrier to communication. With this new information, we may expand the definition of sacrifice to include the 'chasing away of spiritual walls'.

Sacrifice in the Judicial system

Crime is often committed by anti-social individuals. Part of the rehabilitation of these individuals is to mandate some form of community service. When these individuals sacrifice (or give), by fulfilling the 'punishment', it makes them more sociable.

Chi, and healing words from an ancient language.
On a scientific level, sacrifice (giving) is associated with increases in the pro-social hormones prolactin and oxytocin. These hormones are also released when we give and/or receive hugs.

To aid communication; God sacrificed His only Son Jesus Christ. Image by Phillip Medhurst.

Private jet. Image by jetrequest.com

Chi, and healing words from an ancient language.

English:	Hope
Igbo:	Nchekwube
Breakdown:	'Nche' (waiting) & 'kwube' (continue speaking)
Comments:	A human being in good mental condition should always have hope. Hope is a very good emotion that is strongly regarded in the Bible. We hope to get somewhere or something in life, but one central thing we want to do when we get there is to communicate with someone, multiple persons or even an object. Hope is also based on previous statements or speech and waiting for those statements/speech to materialize.

English:	Patience
Igbo:	Ndidi
Breakdown:	'N' (prefix) & 'di' (to be) & 'di' (to be)
Comments:	Patience as a state of being your true self and remaining your true self despite unfavorable environmental challenges. The person who is patient does not respond negatively to unfavorable personal circumstances. Stand your ground, and be strong like a tree. Do not whine. Be resistant to wire- brushing. Be of service, and weather the storm.

English:	Sorry
Igbo:	Ndo
Breakdown:	'N' (verb intensifier) and 'udo' (peace)
Comments:	To pacify; this word is the application of peace to someone. This word is also related to ndo (shelter). To say sorry (ndo) is to bring peace into the consciousness of the offended.

Chi, and healing words from an ancient language.

English:	Peace
Igbo:	udo
Breakdown:	'u' (community prefix) & 'do' (keep)
Comments:	The word for sorry 'ndo' is from the same root. When you keep what you have, you are in peace. There is no peace when we can't keep what belongs to us. The only way we can prosper is through peace, and keeping our possessions. In the Hebrew language, the word for peace, shalom, also means prosperity. Peace is very good for the Chi.

English:	Happiness
Igbo:	Añuli
Breakdown:	'Añu'(honey) & 'li'(eat)
Comments:	Eating honey brings us to an emotional state that approximates happiness. We know that when we feel emotionally low, we tend to uplift ourselves with sugar rich foods such as chocolate. Unfortunately, this type of 'happiness' is temporary, and may expose us to addiction to these sugar rich foods. Fortunately, there are natural things we can do to raise our emotional state such as engaging in a sporting activity or listening to music. When we are truly happy, we feel like we have 'eaten honey', even though we haven't.

English:	Love
Igbo:	Ifunanya.
Breakdown:	'I' (strongly positive) & 'fu'(to see) & 'na' (in) 'anya' (eye)
Comments:	Love is a very interesting topic. In Igbo love is very simple. People in love see things, basically, in the same way. So if they see a painting, they tend to agree as to whether that painting is good or bad. They see things as if they 'borrowed' each other's eyes. They are often in agreement in what they see or perceive. The stronger the agreement, the stronger the love.

People in love like to talk about their perceptions and experiences. Because they have a high level of agreement, they validate each other's perceptions and experiences. This validation, increases the love. This is true whether the love is between two people in an intimate relationship or whether we are referring to a group.

While many people struggle to love, some individuals just love everybody. These individuals appear to have the 'eye of God'.

Love is associated with the highest quality perceptions and thought. The thought is based on the reality of life. Individuals in 'lust' have poor quality thought and perceptions and this explains why such relationships are marred with difficulties.

Dr. Creflo Dollar felt the love of God when he was hugged by fellow Christians at a Bible study group, after he got born again. Those Christians viewed him with the 'eye of God', and loved him from God's perspective. It was a special moment in his life.

To summarize; love is the greatest emotion and is associated with the purest thought and perception. Negative emotions such as anger, jealousy, and unforgiveness disrupt love and affect the quality of our thoughts.

The Human Chi is in the best possible condition when it is filled with love. Love is the 'oil' of the Chi.

Positive Emotions	Negative Emotions
Love	Anger
Joy	Pain
Happiness	Jealousy
Hope	Grief
Faith	Apathy

Love is the greatest emotion and is associated with pure thought. Negative emotions disrupt pure thought. Where love exists, communication and agreement abounds.

Chi, and healing words from an ancient language.

These twins spontaneously fixed each other's ties. They preached together that night and have pretty much the same view of life. That's love.

Self help words

English:	Question
Igbo:	Jụ
Breakdown:	jụ (no)
Comments:	When you question someone, you are basically saying 'no' to whatever they are communicating. Either because there are omissions in their communication, or the subject was not properly communicated. An individual questioning you is basically saying no to what you are communicating. jụ is also the word for cold. Being cold to someone is a way of saying 'no' to them. Some types of cold food are, basically, saying 'no'. See also questioning-ajụjụ

English:	Questioning
Igbo:	Ajụjụ
Breakdown:	'a'(neutral prefix) & 'jụ'(no) & 'ju' (no)
Comments:	Questioning is a way of repeatedly saying 'no' to whatever an individual is communicating. This could be due to omissions or commissions in the communication of the person being questioned.
	For example, a Policeman who is playing soccer, in uniform, could be questioned by a civilian if he was a Policeman. This is a way of saying 'no' to what the irresponsible policeman is communicating.

English:	Help
Igbo:	Aka
Breakdown:	aka (hand)
Comments:	When we get 'help', we are being given a 'hand'.

English:	Slap
Igbo:	Aka-nti
Breakdown:	'aka' (help) & 'nti' (ear)
Comments:	Slapping someone in the modern world can be considered a physical assault. However, it may be appropriate to slap an individual who refuses to obey a verbal command. Women can be placed in such positions by poorly trained men. In such cases, a slap serves as 'help for the ears'. Incidentally, the hand lands next to the ears in a slap as 'hand in the ears'.

English:	Clothing
Igbo:	Akwa
Breakdown:	'a' (negative prefix) & 'kwa'(cry, weep)
Comments:	Clothing creates the opposite of 'cry' which is comfort. In 2015, the global textile industry is expected to be worth $1,557.1 billion. Even in very warm countries and territories, clothing is popular because it induces comfort. Addiction Physicians often encounter patients who go on a

Chi, and healing words from an ancient language.

shopping spree with money they do not have. These patients often have emotional problems such as depression and may be inappropriately trying to obtain 'comfort' from clothing.

English:	Bag
Igbo:	Akpa
Breakdown:	'a'&' kpa'(burden, bother)
Comments:	'a' creates the negative-that which prevents something or items from being burdensome. A bag is a way to put things together so they are not bothersome or difficult to carry.

A bag is used to carry items comfortably.

Chi, and healing words from an ancient language.

English:	We
Igbo:	anyi
Breakdown:	'a' (negative prefix) 'nyi' (beyond)
Comments:	This word illustrates that 'nothing is beyond us'. When we function as a group, we can achieve all things. It may not happen overnight, but we have the power to make it happen. That's why it is beneficial to join groups.

English:	Favor
Igbo:	arinze
Breakdown:	'ari' (suffering)& 'nze' (shepherd priest)
Comments:	This is one the words that is truly empowering. This word suggests that in ancient Igbo society, most people were self sufficient. Ordinarily, people did not request or obtain favor from one another. This does not mean that the people did not help themselves. The word for help is quite different from the word for favor. Favors were more readily obtained from the Nze priests. A favor causes an Nze some suffering. Every favor has a price tag, and it is the Nze who pays. These priests most likely are individuals who made great sacrifices for the community. Even in the modern world, Christian priests are in good positions to help people in need. When one is looking for a job, it makes sense to talk to a priest who may know someone that may help.

English:	Spit
Igbo:	Aṣọ
Breakdown:	'a' (negative prefix) & 'ṣọ'(to respect) 'a' creates the negative.
Comments:	To disrespect, to deconsecrate. See also nsọ- reverence.

Chi, and healing words from an ancient language.

English:	End
Igbo:	Chi
Breakdown:	Chi=end
Comments:	Chi means end. We note it in certain words such as uzoechina (let the road not end) or obiechina (let the house not end). We also use it in the word for Chi (personal guardian). Chi is a spiritual and emotional complex of an individuals spirit, mind, and body. Its condition determines our failures and successes. At the end of the day, our 'Chi' is ultimately in charge. The Chi is the end. God is the Alpha and omega.

English:	Coronation/Crowning
Igbo:	Chi
Breakdown:	Chi=end
Comments:	Chi is also used to describe coronation. When an individual is crowned with a title, it represents an 'end point' for the person. In reality, there is really no end. An end is always the beginning of something new.

English:	Thank You
Igbo:	Dalụ
Breakdown:	'da' (keep) & 'lụ' (work)
Comments:	Saying 'thank you' is a way of telling someone 'keep working'. Every human being is here to provide some type of service for his fellow human beings. When we do something good and someone says thank you, that's a tacit encouragement for us to 'keep working'.

English:	Being, well being.
Igbo:	Di
Breakdown:	di-to be.
Comments:	See forgiveness below.

Chi, and healing words from an ancient language.

English:	Dance, Game(play)
Igbo:	Egwu
Breakdown:	'e' (prefix used as a partial positive) & 'gwu' (to protect). See ugwu (hill)
Comments:	Dance is basically a game. The purpose of a game is to protect our spirit, so we can play more games. Igbo understood that life is like a game with goals and obstructions. Although we may experience major painful events like loosing a job, but life remains basically like a game. Sometimes we get disillusioned, and give up our dreams and goals, because we have judged the barriers insurmountable. We may feel like we are playing against a major football athlete. Dance (egwu) is a game (egwu) that can rehabilitate and protect our spirit, so we can get back into the game of life. We naturally tend to break into a dance when we score a goal in a sport (notice the hard work required to score a goal), because dance is naturally linked to achieving goals. When we dance frequently, we would probably score more goals, in sports and in general life. Dance is very good for the Chi (personal spiritual guardian). Dance moves the Chi to more positive emotional states such as love and joy.

Chi, and healing words from an ancient language.

Woman uses dance to rehabilitate her body, mind and spirit. The man uses a metal gong to encourage her.

English:	Game
Igbo:	Egwu
Breakdown:	'e' (prefix used as a partial negative) & 'gwu' (to protect). See ugwu (hill)
Comments:	Life is a game. In life we ordinarily have goals. A general goal could be to grow old. This goal, off-course, has several limitations. It means we need to get a good job,

Chi, and healing words from an ancient language.

have healthy relationships and eat healthy. Because life
can be challenging, and we may not readily achieve our
goals, this may cost us some esteem. For instance, we
may lose valuable people in our lives due to sickness
and death.

Naturally, these losses make us feel emotionally 'low'.
One way to protect our spirit, so we can keep playing
the game of life, is to play games such as soccer or
chess. These games (e.g. soccer or chess) expose us to
the concept of win and loss in games, and all the
emotions associated with it.

Games are good for the Chi.

Chess. Image by Michael Maggs.

English:	Helping
Igbo:	Enyemaka
Breakdown:	enye (to give) & aka (hand)
Comments:	Help is giving someone a hand.

Chi, and healing words from an ancient language.

English:	Friend
Igbo:	Enyi
Breakdown:	"e"(partial positive)& "nyi"(variant of nye-give)
Comments:	A friend is a giver. This is someone who positively contributes to your existence. A friend gives good advice and supports your activities. One common mistake is to have associates that are not friendly. This is a first-class ticket to heart-break.

English:	Good
Igbo:	Ezigbo
Breakdown:	'e'(partial positive) & 'zi'(reveal) & 'gbo' (protect, guard)
Comments:	Guarding and protection is a strong theme in Igbo life. The verb 'gbo' is also seen in the word Igbo. In order for anyone or anything to survive and flourish they need some type of protection. A good person is a revelation of some form of protection. A person who is good to us, is protecting us from something that is evil. For example, a partner could be protecting us from loneliness, and we may not quickly appreciate it.

English:	Truth
Igbo:	Eziokwu
Breakdown:	'e'(partial positive) & 'zi'(show, reveal) & okwu (speech)
Comments:	What comes out of an individual's mouth can either be truthful or misleading. Truth is speech that is revealing. Truth shows us the way.

Chi, and healing words from an ancient language.

English:	Change
Igbo:	gbanwe
Breakdown:	gba (apply) & 'nwe' (own)
Comments:	To change is to 'apply ownership'. When I change my shirt, I am applying my ownership of shirts. Sometimes people in a relationship or in a work place change. People can be distressed when this happens. One of the reasons they change is that there has been some change of ownership. Sometimes people don't show their true color because they are afraid they will lose a job or a partner. When they re-gain ownership of themselves, they quickly change.

English:	Stupidity, moronic behavior
Igbo:	Nsọkwu
Breakdown:	'Nsọ'(respect, reverence) & 'kwu' (speech)
Comments:	Stupid people have a 'reverence for words'. They are at the command of other peoples words. If you tell them to 'come over here'. They sheepishly come. If you tell them, 'they are stupid'; they act stupid. These people can easily be manipulated with words. A word like the 'n' word can drive them into uncontrollable rage. The real problem is not necessarily the words, but the negative emotions associated with the words. For example, a verbal insult may lead to emotional pain. The verbal insult and the emotional pain becomes registered in the memory. That emotional pain can be replayed consciously or unconsciously. Emotional pain is very bad for the Chi, and hinders progress. Fortunately, the Igbo have the technology to deactivate the words.

Chi, and healing words from an ancient language.

English:	Trouble
Igbo:	Nsogbu
Breakdown:	'Nso'(following)& 'gbu' (pain)
Comments:	Trouble seems to arise when people sub-consciously follow pain. When we are inflicted with physical or emotional pain it depresses our consciousness. Once depressed, we can be sub-consciously controlled by our pain without our express knowledge. Chronic pain then causes misjudgments that can bring us trouble. When we get into trouble in life, it is helpful to look inwards into the pains of our lives. A registered therapist can help us eradicate the pain, and the accompanying trouble.

English:	Curse, cursing
Igbo:	Ibụ-ọnụ
Breakdown:	Ibụ (being) & ọnụ (mouth)
Comments:	We have already learnt that there is power in the spoken word. Truly, words can exert incredible power. This is because the mind requires information from our memory and experiences to function. Words by themselves do not have any real power. If you doubt me, put up your hands in front of someone who is speaking and find out for yourself if those words have power. The power of words lies in our memories and experiences. The emotions associated with the words, exaggerates its power. When we believe the word of God, then it has power because it is active in our memories and is associated with good feelings and emotions. The same thing applies to curses, we give it power. Anyone, who seems to be under a curse, is just living out some other persons 'mouth'. Therapists can be helpful in identifying the words used in a curse so that novel ways of deactivating them can be achieved. Part of the reason words have so much power is that words in our memories are associated with emotions and negative feelings. For example, someone could say something to someone

that is offensive which causes emotional pain. Whenever the person replays those words in their minds, consciously or unconsciously, they re-live the emotional pain. Overtime, chronically replayed, these words can make us unhappy by inducing emotional pain.

Pain is an emotional state that affects the quality of our thoughts and hampers our progress. See stupidity (nsọkwu).

To summarize; the negative emotions and feelings associated with curses affect the quality of our thoughts and can impede someone's progress in life. One way to counter the negative emotions associated with curses is to feed the soul with positive ones. Christianity has numerous positive statements that are good for the soul;

- You may not know Me, but I know everything about you. Psalm 139: 1
- I know when you sit down and when your rise up. Psalm 139: 2.
- I am familiar with all your ways. Psalm 139: 2
- Even the very hairs on your head are numbered. Matthew 10: 29-31.
- For you were made in my image. Genesis 1: 27
- In Me you live and move and have your being. Acts 17: 28.
- For you are My offspring. Acts 17: 28.
- I knew you even before you were conceived. Jeremiah 1: 4-5.
- I chose you when I planned creation. Ephesians 1: 11-12.
- You were not a mistake for all your days are written in My book. Psalm 139: 15-16.
- I determined the exact time of your birth and where you would live. Acts 17: 26.
- You are fearfully and wonderfully made. Psalm 139: 14.
- I knit you together in your mother's womb. Psalm 139: 13.
- And brought you forth on the day you were born. Psalm 71: 6.

Chi, and healing words from an ancient language.

- I have been misrepresented by those who do not know me. John 8: 41-44.
- I am not distant and angry, but am the complete expression of love. 1 John 4: 16.
- And it is my desire to lavish my love on you. 1 John 3: 1.
- I offer you more than your earthly father ever could. Matthew 7: 11.
- For I am the perfect father. Matthew 5: 48.
- Every good gift that you receive comes from my hand. James 1: 17.
- For I AM your provider and I meet all your needs. Matthew 6: 31-33.
- My plan for you future has always been filled with hope. Jeremiah 29: 11.
- Because I love you with an everlasting love. Jeremiah 31: 3.
- My thoughts toward you are countless as the sand on the seashore. Psalm 139: 17-18.
- And I rejoice over you with singing. Zephaniah 3: 17.
- I will never stop doing good to you. Jeremiah 32: 41.
- And I want to show you great and marvelous things. Jeremiah 33: 3.
- If you seek me with all your heart you will find me. Deuteronomy 4: 29.
- Delight in me and I will give you the desires of your heart. Psalm 37: 4.
- For it is I who gave you those desires. Philippians 2: 13.
- I am able to do more for you than you could possibly imagine. Ephesians 3: 20.
- For I Am your greatest encourager. 2 Thessalonians 2: 16-17.
- I AM also the father who comforts you in all your troubles. 2 Corinthians 1: 3-4.
- When you are broken, I am close to you. Psalm 34: 18.
- As a shepherd carries a lamb, I have carried you close to my heart. Isaiah 40: 11.
- One day I will wipe away every tear from your eyes. Revelations 21: 3-4.

  More at www.fathersloveletter.com

Chi, and healing words from an ancient language.

Curses have to be deactivate in order to return the chi to an optimum condition.

English:	Because
Igbo:	Maka
Breakdown:	'Ma' (know, knowledge) & 'ka' (greater)
Comments:	In life, some events happen in a sequence caused by a preceding event. The preceding event is a greater phenomenon or a greater knowledge. For example, a dude crashes into a wedding party because he expects to find single girls there. The single girls is a greater than the wedding party.

English:	Solution
Igbo:	Igbo-mkpa
Breakdown:	'igbo' (prevent, guard) & 'mkpa' (bother, thorn, burden)
Comments:	A problem is something that is bothersome. It is a thorn and a burden to our existence. A solution to a problem begins with an understanding of how the problem bothers us. Armed with this information we can go ahead and device means to prevent it from bothering us. For example, if you do not have a job, one of the first things to do is to make a list of how not having a job is adversely affecting you. Things on the list could be; -inability to pay school loans. -inability to take care of parents and loved ones. -inability to utilize the knowledge you gained from school. -inability to travel and enjoy life. -etc Armed with this information one can device novel ways to approach hiring managers in order to solve these problems. In science, a problem statement is a pre-requisite of a solution.

Chi, and healing words from an ancient language.

English:	Singing
Igbo:	Igụ egwu
Breakdown:	'igụ' (hunger) & 'egwu' (dance)
Comments:	A song is used to induce a 'hunger for dance'. Dance was used to rehabilitate the body, the mind, and the spirit. The spirit perpetually seeks higher levels of comfort and entertainment. This is why in Christianity, we hope to go to heaven by abiding to the teachings of Christ. Heaven is the highest level of comfort and entertainment possible. While on earth, the spirit seeks comfort and entertainment as well, but this cannot be attained without a healthy body and mind. Dance is one of the interventions that was developed, thousands of years ago, to help in the restoration of the body, the mind, and the spirit to higher levels. Music is good for the Chi.

English:	Singing
Igbo:	Ikwe ukwe
Breakdown:	'Ikwe' (reinforce) & 'u'(prefix) & 'kwe' (agree)
Comments:	A song is used to 'reinforce an agreement'. This is often used spiritually. Humans are inherently weak spiritually that's why God sent us the holy spirit. When we take our agreements of our belief in God and put it into a song, it's a way to 'reinforce that agreement'. That's why in Churches, songs are an important component of a service. It is definitely a way to help us align more with the spirit (thought) of God.

English:	Power
Igbo:	Ike
Breakdown:	'I'(positive prefix) & 'ke'(create)
Comments:	Power is creation. Power is the ability to create. An individual with power is able to change the physical universe into a desired structure such as buildings. They can create jobs. They have wide powers to create. Sometimes, individuals in power can create war that leads to suffering and destruction. Unfortunately, that ugly situation is still a creation.

Chi, and healing words from an ancient language.

English:	First (being first)
Igbo:	Ibụzọ
Breakdown:	'Ibụ' (being) & 'ụzọ' (way)
Comments:	When we are 'first' in any human activity, we are being the 'way'. We are essentially opening a 'way' in the realms of that human activity or endeavor. Whenever we are first, it calls for great responsibility.

English:	Last (being last)
Igbo:	Ikpeazụ
Breakdown:	'Ikpe'(reporting) & 'azụ' (back)
Comments:	The person who is at the back has the advantage of the rear view. That person can give an account of what is happening at the back which the people in front are not privy. Being last is not necessarily a bad thing. There is a saying that "he who laughs last, laughs best".

English:	Reverence
Igbo:	Nsọ
Breakdown:	'N' (prefix) & 'sọ' (respect or reverence.)
Comments:	See asọ (spit)

English:	Misfortune
Igbo:	ọdachi
Breakdown:	'ọda' (fall) & 'chi' (end)
Comments	Death is a misfortune. It represents the 'fall of the end'. A misfortune brings an end to some event or activity. A loss of ones job is also an odachi. It is the 'fall of the end' in income generation from that job source.

Chi, and healing words from an ancient language.

Forgiveness technology

English:	Forgive, Forgiveness
Igbo:	gbahalụ
Breakdown:	'gba' (apply) & 'halụ' (leave it alone)
Comments:	Many people confess that forgiveness is very difficult. Sometimes a conflict has lingered for so long that forgiveness may seem impossible. Forgiveness between the Arabs and the Israelis may seem to be a far-fetched idea. Fortunately, forgiveness is something we must be able to do if we are to achieve health, love and happiness. While love and happiness are positive emotions, unforgiveness is a negative one. One of the features of love as recorded in 1 Corinthians 13 verse 5 is that it 'keeps no record of wrongs'.
	One of the reasons forgiveness is a challenge is because it requires active mental work. In Igbo, forgiveness is achieved by 'applying' the concept of 'leave it alone'. To forgive, we must mentally figure out what is causing the unforgiveness, then learn to 'leave it alone'.
	Unforgiveness is one of the bad emotions that prevent us from remaining in the highest living state possible- the state of love. It is helpful to understand the four types of forgetting in Igbo-ichefu, ilofu, ilozo an ichezo. They can certainly help in 'leaving things alone'.
	Forgiveness is more easily said than done and it is understandably quite difficult to achieve. Other healthy ways of achieving forgiveness are therefore recommended.
	One can engage in activities that turn on more positive emotions such as happiness and peace. Some of these activities are exercise, dance, singing, prayer, worship or studying the Bible or Word of God.
	Forgiveness is very good for the Chi. When we forgive we get rid of negative emotions associated with unforgiveness.
	Forgiveness makes us feel better; much better than revenge.

Chi, and healing words from an ancient language.

English:	Forgive, forgiveness
Igbo:	"Di", "die", "Idi"
Breakdown:	di=being=living
Comments:	To forgive is to be the person you were pre-mental injury or emotional assault. To forgive is to recover emotionally and psychological to the point that you are who you were before the challenge. This also means that you recover completely to your original state, so that a repeat of the challenge is not possible. Anyone on this planet hoping to be well without forgiveness, might as well be wasting his/her time. Forgiveness is living.

English:	Forgetting
Igbo:	Ichefu
Breakdown:	'iche' (thinking) & 'fu' (throw away)
Comments:	In this type of forgetting, a person is deliberately throwing away useless thoughts. This is a fully conscious individual, who is not suppressing or denying harmful thoughts. This is very useful in forgiveness. For example, a person practices throwing away negative thoughts, such as an experience with an abusive spouse.

English:	Forgetting
Igbo:	ichezo
Breakdown:	'iche' (thinking) & 'zo' (road, save)
Comments:	The purpose of a road is to create a safe short cut between two points. In Ichezo, we deliberately jump from one thought to another by building a road in our thoughts. The intentions is to by-pass painful thoughts or emotions. This type of forgetting is useful in forgiveness. For example, a friend of mine always remembers his ex-wife with some bitterness. So he learnt to build a road in his thoughts by remembering a period they were happy together. He would practice remembering her, then quickly go to a place they were happy together. He is quickly replacing a

Chi, and healing words from an ancient language.

	potentially depressing thought, with one with more pleasant sensations. If you were thinking: "oh this sounds like Jesus'" love your enemy". You are right! Hate is a negative emotion, that is very bad for the Chi. Building a way to more pleasant emotions in ones thought, is a practical way to love an 'enemy'.

English:	Forgetting
Igbo:	Ilofu
Breakdown:	'Ilo' (postulation) & 'fu' (throwing away)
Comments:	In this higher form of forgetting, the spirit is responsible for the action. Here the spirit deliberately throws away 'negative thoughts' before making a postulate. This is very useful in forgiveness. In this case, a postulate does not include considerations from painful memories. For example, a woman says I like that tall guy, but tall guys always cheat. The postulate; 'tall guys always cheat' needs to be thrown away.

English:	Forgetting
Igbo:	Ilozo
Breakdown:	'Ilo'(postulate) & 'zo' (road)
Comments:	In this type of forgetting, the spirit deliberately goes through a road in the memory lane in order to come up with a healthy postulate. Bad painful memories are by-passed. This is obviously healthy for the mind and is good for forgiveness. For example, a woman was struggling to forgive her husband who crashed her car 6 months ago. Her husband borrowed her car 3 hours ago, and she says; "my husband is with my car, and he learns from his mistakes, so he is going to be here soon".

To have a good Chi, having a highly developed forgiveness technology is a must.

The Chi

The Chi is a personal spiritual force that guides a given individual. It is a summation of the emotional forces operating in the individual. A person with a good Chi has an abundance of love, joy, happiness, peace and other positive emotions. A preponderance of anger, jealousy, revenge, sadness and other negative emotions leads to misfortune.

The Chi can be considered a direct extension of the spirit of God into every individual. It is a mechanism of contact and communication.

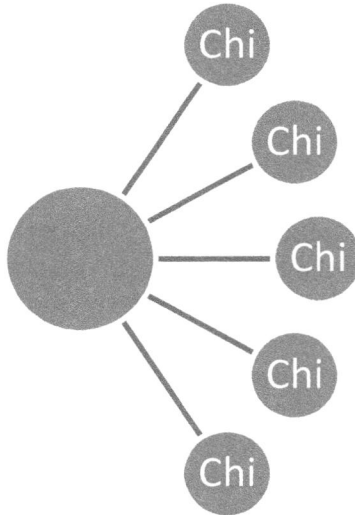

Chi-ukwu (Big Chi) is God, and extends to every human being.

Chi, and healing words from an ancient language.

Activities and agents that can create a good Chi.

Several factors affect the state of the Chi. The following factors could lead to a more desirable Chi status;

- Attending Church services and other activities that lead to worshipping God. God is love, so worshipping God draws us closer to the state of love.
- Forgiveness make us shed the negative emotions associated with lack of forgiveness.
- Sacrifice through giving in your religious organization or volunteering in a soup kitchen or similar organizations can help in creating a good Chi. Sacrifice is known to increase the secretion of the pro-social hormones prolactin and oxytocin.
- Physical activity: cycling, swimming, jogging, running, strolling, gardening and other physical activities are good for the Chi.
- Music and dance.
- Celestial body consciousness-paying attention to the position of the sun, moon and stars whenever possible.
- Healing breath-slow deep breaths can boost our energy levels and help fight negative emotions.
- Therapy, by a registered therapists, is helpful by tackling past traumatic experiences that add sorrow to our Chi.
- Healthy food is excellent for the chi.
- Herbs such as rhodiola and valerian may help create healthier emotions.
- Drugs such as anxiolytics, and anti-depressants have been shown to be helpful in creating positive emotions.
- Ochi (Cupping) is an ancient procedure practiced around the world. In Igbo it is called Ichi Ochi. Generally, there is the dry and wet cupping. In dry cupping, cuts are not made on the skin. In wet cupping, cuts are made on the skin of the desired area. Using a silicone or glass device, suction is applied on the area. Variations of the procedure include applying white chalk (nzu) and pepper.

Chi, and healing words from an ancient language.

The procedure is very popular in China and the Middle- East and is commonly known as Cupping. In ancient Igbo, animal horns were used to provide suction. Animal horns are not used in modern cupping. Several studies suggest that Cupping is efficacious in some medical conditions.

Ancient cupping with an animal horn. Image courtesy of KIT.

Chi, and healing words from an ancient language.

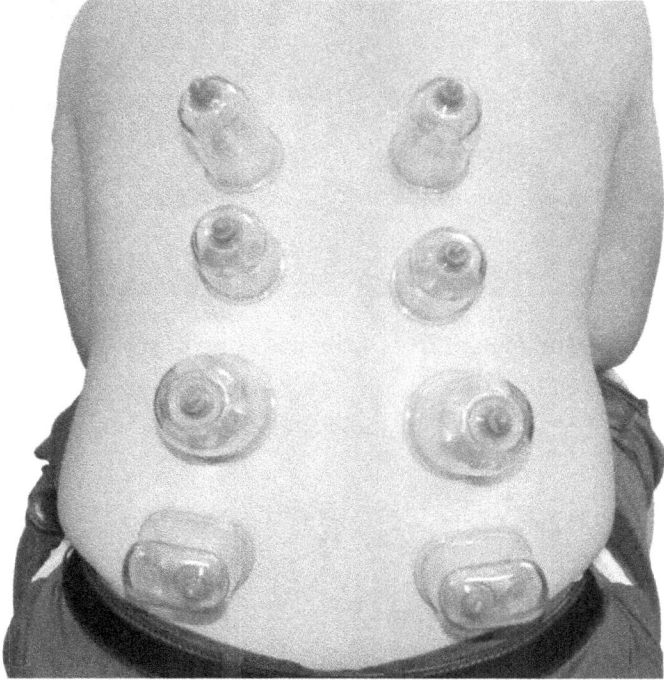

Modern cupping.

Obviously, in order to maintain a good Chi, one should avoid sinful and other self-destructive behaviors.

Chi, and healing words from an ancient language.

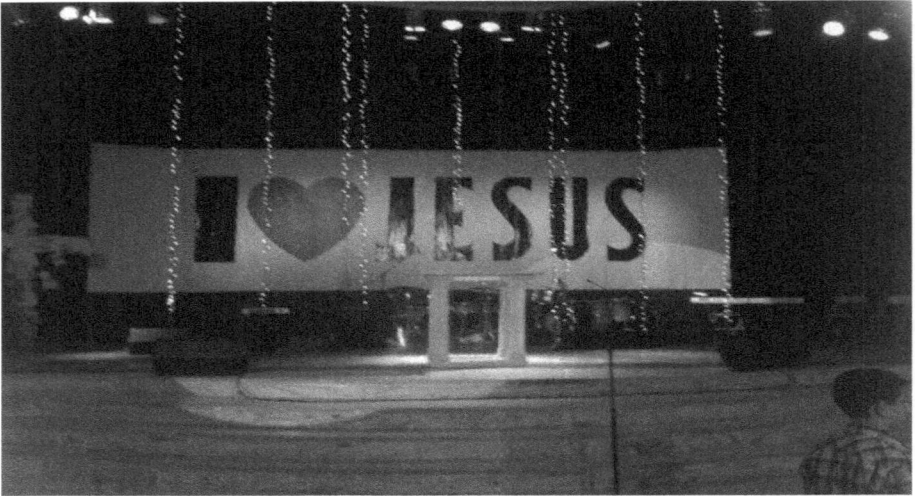

Connecting with God in a place of worship is one of the best ways of creating a positive Chi.

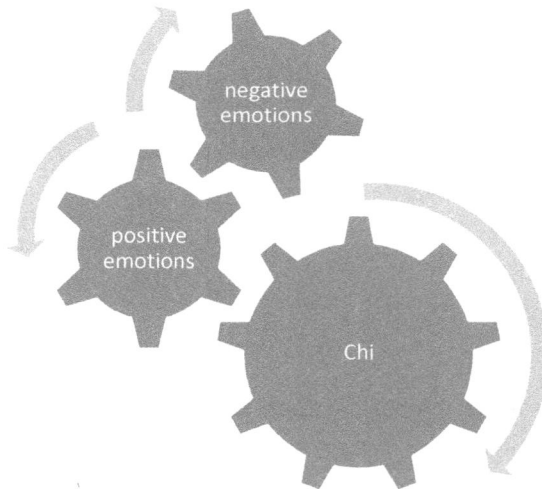

The Chi: negative emotions such as anger and frustration work against the Chi.

Chi, and healing words from an ancient language.

Spirituality

English:	My body
Igbo:	arụ mụ
Breakdown:	'arụ' (body) & 'mụ' (my soul)
Comments:	I am not my body. It is just the body (covering) of my soul. See also onwe mu(owner of my soul or my spirit). Basically, humans are spirit which operate through a soul and body. (also see 1 Thessalonians 5: 23)

English:	My soul or mind
Igbo:	Mụ
Breakdown:	Mụ=learn
Comments:	The soul is used to compute everyday problems. The soul has access to the memory with all the stored experiences. Its main function is learning. It uses the stored information to avoid painful mistakes and create good opportunities for the spirit and body. onwe mụ (owner of my soul) is the spirit. See also my body (arụ mụ).

English:	Spirit
Igbo:	Mmụọ
Breakdown:	'M' (positive prefix) & mụ (my soul) & 'ọ' (personal suffix)
Comments:	Each human is a spirit which possesses a soul. The spirit controls a body through the soul in normal circumstances.

English:	My spirit
Igbo:	onwe-mụ
Breakdown:	'onwe' (owner) & 'mụ' (my soul)
Comments:	The spirit is the owner of my soul or my mind. I am not my body. I am not my soul. I am my spirit. My spirit uses my soul and body to do the tasks it chooses.

Chi, and healing words from an ancient language.

English:	Pagan prosperity deity
Igbo:	Agwu
Breakdown:	'a'(negative prefix) & 'gwu'(finish)
Comments:	That which cannot finish-a source of abundance. Some individuals believed that this deity could provide them with abundant material resources. Christianity teaches that Jesus is the only way.

English:	Law
Igbo:	Iwu
Breakdown:	'I' (strongly positive prefix) & 'wu'(agony)
Comments:	The verb 'wu' is seen in agony (owu) and prolonged agony (nwute). When one violates the law, agony is experienced. Just being stopped by a traffic cop for over-speeding may cause agony, even if a ticket is not issued.

English:	Abomination
Igbo:	Alu
Breakdown:	'a' (negative prefix) & 'lu' (to make, to work or create)
Comments:	To undo or destroy something made. 'a' creates the negative. Society is like a machine with many gears working towards a common goal. To commit an abomination, is to destroy this machinery. Fortunately, an abomination can be repaired through God's grace. Alu (abomination) can be considered as the opposite of olu (work).

English:	Prophesy
Igbo:	Amuma
Breakdown:	'a' (negative prefix) & 'ma'(to know) & 'uma' (to know)-- here 'a' also creates the negative. 'U' is an amplilifier/intensifier.
Comments:	To know the future without current knowledge. This word suggests that all a prophet does is to create a future situation by word of mouth. This is commonly an individual, with an exceptional knowledge of God and society that can capture a future condition in 'words'.

Chi, and healing words from an ancient language.

English:	Beauty, good.
Igbo:	Mma
Breakdown:	Mma is to know.
Comments:	Beauty is a statement of good knowledge. A beautiful car is a statement of good knowledge of cars. A beautiful woman is an expression of good knowledge of femininity. Knowledge is good or beautiful.

English:	Bless
Igbo:	Gọzie
Breakdown:	'gọ' (relate) & 'zie' (demonstrate)
Comments:	The verb 'gọ' is used in the word for in-law (ọgọ) and in the word for denial 'agọ'. To bless or be blessed is to demonstrate a relationship.

English:	Denial
Igbo:	Agọ
Breakdown:	'a' (negative prefix) & 'gọ' (relate)
Comments:	The verb 'gọ' is used in the word for in-law (ọgọ) and in the word for bless 'gọzie'. Denial is dismantling of a relationship.

English:	Prayer
Igbo:	Ekpele
Breakdown:	'e'(partial positive prefix) + ' kpe'(communicate, report)& 'le'(happen, actualize, manifest)
Comments:	Prayer contains two main elements-communication and manifestation. 'e' creates a partial positive (muffling), suggesting that the focus is on manifestation. Prayer in Igbo is in agreement with the Nike ad "Just do it". In Igbo; you kneel and meditate. Do not whine to God like a little kid. Go out there and 'just do it!!' See also knee (Ikpele).

Chi, and healing words from an ancient language.

English:	Crouch
Igbo:	Sekpuluana
Breakdown:	'se' (draw) & 'kpulu' (cover) & 'ana' (earth)
Comments:	In everyday speech, we translate this word as kneeling but it is a different posture. This is the posture one assumes when an individual is trying to pray. In this position, after kneeling, the head is bowed to the same level as the ground or bed. It looks like the person is covering the earth, or is like a 'hat' over the earth. Note that Okpu (hat) is from kpu (cover).

Crouching in prayer.

Chi, and healing words from an ancient language.

English:	Devil
Igbo:	Ekwensu
Breakdown:	'e' (partial negative) & 'kwe' (agree) & ' n' (prefix) & 'su' (to breakdown)= refuses breakdown=obstacle
Comments:	Although some individuals are scared of the devil, but this should not be the case. While the Bible notes that the devil is a defeated foe, Igbo seems to agree. Basically, the devil is the one who prevents us from achieving our objectives. We achieve our objectives when we become stronger than the obstacles . The devil is the obstacle that is resisting breaking down. He is making things hard for us. In ancient Igbo, ekwensu was often invoked during wars, as a 'god of war'.

English:	Excommunication
Igbo:	Mmachi
Breakdown:	'mma' (to know) & 'chi' (end).
Comments:	Excommunication is the end of one's life as they knew it. Excommunication can be temporary.

English:	Fine
Igbo:	Nra
Breakdown:	'N' (positive prefix) & 'ra'(to leave)
Comments:	Fines can be used to enforce laws in any community. A fine indicates that you have to 'leave' something that belonged to you. The pain associated with the loss is expected to be a deterrent towards further violation of the law.

English:	Masquerade
Igbo:	Mmọnwụ
Breakdown:	'Mma' + 'onwụ'
Comments:	Mma (good, beautiful) & onwụ (death)- that which beautifies death. Masquerades are often called to perform during burial ceremonies. They are, supposedly, the spirit of departed ancestors. Their agility, dance, and movements suggest that though one is dead physically, they are very much alive and active, in the spiritual.

Chi, and healing words from an ancient language.

English:	Praise, praise worship
Igbo:	Otuto
Breakdown:	'otu'(group) & 'to' (praise)
Comments:	Praise is an 'oneness' activity to recognize an individual or God. A church choir is, basically, performing 'group praise'.

English:	Sun bathing
Igbo:	Nyalụ anwụ
Breakdown:	'Nyalụ' (carry, ride) & 'anwụ' (sun)
Comments:	Sunshine is associated with happiness. Sun bathing allows us to make Vitamin D in the skin which supports healthy bones and strengthens our immune system. From a distance, sunbathing looks like carrying the sun.

Women sunbathing appear to be 'carrying' the sun.

Chi, and healing words from an ancient language.

English:	Salvation
Igbo:	Nzọpụta
Breakdown:	'nzọ' (to save) & 'pụta' (outing)
Comments:	Salvation is 'saving out' an individual from death or destruction.

English:	Stepping out
Igbo:	Nzọpụta
Breakdown:	'Nzọ' (stepping) & 'pụta' (out)
Comments:	This may be related to salvation because personal action is required in salvation. The first action is, stepping out of one's comfort zone, in a Church or religious venue to receive salvation.

English:	Igbo staff of Authority.
Igbo:	ọffọr (ọfọ)
Breakdown:	'ọ' (personal prefix) & 'fọ' (to remain)
Comments:	The ọffọr is the Igbo staff of authority. It is derived from a branch of a special tree. The holder of an ọfọ is expected to speak the truth at all times. The truth is what sets us free. It is symbolic, and derived from the fact that the branches of a tree cause it to remain standing. The person who speaks the truth will remain standing. Be like a tree; branch out or diversify. Do not depend on one primary branch for survival. When you are diversified, you will not be afraid to speak the truth for fear of losing a job or a relationship.

Chi, and healing words from an ancient language.

To guarantee long term survival, a tree depends on several branches.

English:	Medicine, drug
Igbo:	ọgwụ
Breakdown:	'ọ' (personal intensifier) and 'gwụ' (finish)
Comments:	Medicine as that which finishes my illnesses. I am only well when my illness is 'finished'. Because when an individuals illness ends, the person gets complete, we can assume 'ọgwụ' also means completion. When an individual is ill, they need their medicine to be complete.

Chi, and healing words from an ancient language.

English:	Sin, misaction
Igbo:	Mmehe
Breakdown:	'Mme'(action) + 'he' (open)
Comments:	Humans are expected to act within certain confines to bring good to themselves and their communities. A sin creates an opening, some sort of pandora box, whose contents are unknown. A sin can be considered a dangerous wide open action, that serves no useful purpose, and can cause harm. A person with a good Chi, avoids wasteful non-purposeful actions.

English:	Corpse
Igbo:	Ozu
Breakdown:	'O' (verb intensifier used on personal issues), & 'zu' (completion, thief)
Comments:	When someone dies, what remains is the corpse. The corpse represents a 'completion' of the cycle of life for the individual. The corpse is also the 'thief' or 'retainer' of the spirit, which escapes when an individual dies. When an individual is alive, the body (the thief) prevents the true essence of the spirit from manifesting. Prayer, meditation and fasting are spiritual tools used to tame the body so the true essence of the spirit is brought to light in one's life time, as much as possible.

Sexuality

Sex is important in the propagation of any community. Lawful and consensual sexual activity is encouraged.

English:	Sex
Igbo:	Ila- ọtụ
Breakdown:	'ila'(to lick) & 'ọtụ'(vagina)
Comments:	In this type of sexual activity, the vagina is 'licked' by any acceptable organ.

Chi, and healing words from an ancient language.

English:	Fornication
Igbo:	Ikwa-iko
Breakdown:	'ikwa'(push) & 'iko'(vagina)
Comments:	The verb 'ko' is seen in the word for cup 'iko'. 'Ko' is the motion to draw or scoop. A cup is used to 'draw' water. The two (cup and vagina) 'ikos' are phonologically slightly different. The vagina has the power to draw wanted and unwanted men. The vagina is considered a type of sacred vessel, that should be honored, and not pushed around with a penis.

Relationships

English:	Wife
Igbo:	Nwunye
Breakdown:	'nwa'(child) & 'unye'(giving)
Comments:	A wife is supposed to receive all kinds of gifts.

English:	Husband
Igbo:	Di
Breakdown:	Di=being=forgiving
Comments:	To live is to forgive. A husband represents being. A woman who has a husband is living.

English:	Mother
Igbo:	Nne
Breakdown:	'n'(prefix) & 'ne'(see or oversee)
Comments:	The mother is a general overseer of the house. Oversees the Children, and the father as well. The father and mother are co-overseers.

Chi, and healing words from an ancient language.

English:	Father
Igbo:	Nna
Breakdown:	'n'(privative) & 'na' (a variant of supervision-see 'nne')
Comments:	'na' is related to 'ne' which refers to see or oversee. A father is an overseer, but it appears that this job function is made possible by the presence or activity of a mother(nne).

English:	Children
Igbo:	ụmụ
Breakdown:	'ụ' (community prefix) & 'mụ' (my soul & learning)
Comments:	The verb 'mụ' is used to describe learning and the soul. Humans use their souls to learn right, wrong, pain or pleasure. Basically, a soul would like to avoid pain and seek pleasure. A soul could pass on what it has learnt through children. Naturally, we guide our children away from our painful mistakes. Children allow us to extend our soul and learning in the community. The use of community prefix 'ụ' suggests that our children, partly, belong to the community. It is good to have children because they serve as our ambassadors when we die.

English:	Human Being, Important human being.
Igbo:	Mmadụ
Breakdown:	mma (knowledge) + "n"dụ (life)= to know life.
Comments:	In Igbo land, an mmadụ (human being, important human being) is a person 'who knows how life is'. This person knows how life works, and is a very good resource when a solution is sought. Individuals who are not aware of their Chi, and who have no spiritual knowledge, may not be qualified as mmadụ. See also beauty (mma).

Chi, and healing words from an ancient language.

English:	Female
Igbo:	Nwanyi
Breakdown:	'Nwa' (child) & 'anyi' (us)
Comments:	A female child is always welcome in the community as 'our child'.

English:	Male
Igbo:	Nwoke
Breakdown:	'Nwa' (child) & 'oke' (creation)
Comments:	A male child creates his own life. He creates his own profession and means of livelihood.

English:	Person
Igbo:	Onye
Breakdown:	'O' (prefix) & 'nye' (giver)
Comments:	'O' is used personally as an intensifier. A person is a giver. People should live in the context that they are givers. Everything alive is providing a service to someone or something else. E.g. a tree provides a service by making a fruit for a monkey, and the monkey disperses the seed of the fruit on behalf of the tree. Every individual should be providing some service or good. A person who is not capable of providing any service might as well be dead. Little children are very valuable because they can give and receive love from their parents.

English:	In-Law
Igbo:	ọgọ
Breakdown:	'ọ' (personal prefix) & 'gọ' (relate=bless)
Comments:	The verb gọ is used in the word bless. In-laws are relations that are inherently a blessing.

Chi, and healing words from an ancient language.

English:	Group, peer group.
Igbo:	Out
Breakdown:	'O' (prefix) & 'tu' (togetherness, oneness)
Comments:	A group is about creating togetherness or oneness. The purpose of a group is to act like one. This is a way to leverage power. If you are having trouble achieving a goal, try joining a group and leverage your power.

English:	Good night
Igbo:	Kachifo
Breakdown:	'Ka' (permit) & 'chi' (end) & 'fo' (withdraw)
Comments:	Darkness represents the end (chi) of the day. In saying goodnight, we are making a wish for the darkness to withdraw, so a new day can show up.

Professions

English:	Work, Job
Igbo:	ọlụ
Breakdown:	'ọ'(personal prefix) & 'lụ' (make)
Comments:	Work is making or creating something. In any job, you can always define what you are making or creating. For instance, I am creating a book that would revolutionize our understanding of the Chi and the Igbo language. I intend this book to create sparks that lights fires around the world.

English:	Hunting
Igbo:	Nta
Breakdown:	'N' (prefix) & 'ta' (bite)
Comments:	When we observe animals hunting in the wild, we notice that a 'bite' wound often subdues the prey. So hunting is basically inducing a 'bite' either with teeth, spear, bullets or any other object. After a successful hunt, people would like to have a 'bite' of the meat, off-course.

Chi, and healing words from an ancient language.

English:	Farm, farming
Igbo:	Ugbo
Breakdown:	'U' (prefix) & 'gbo' (prevent, guarding)
Comments:	'U' is an intensifier often used when the activity refers to more than one person (community activity). Farming as a preventive measure. It protects against scarcity of food and starvation. Farm today and eat tomorrow. The same verb 'gbo' is used in Igbo (the language and people). Prevention and protection is a strong theme in Igbo and the Chi.

English:	Doctor, medicine-man
Igbo:	Dibia
Breakdown:	'di' (well being) & 'bia' (come)
Comments:	A medicine-man is someone who brings well being. This is true of doctors in the modern world. A central part of well being is forgiveness. The same verb that describes well being also portrays forgiveness. People like Adolf Hitler, who was on multiple Psychiatric medications, cannot be well, because they cannot forgive. I'd like to consider forgiveness a selfish move to protect an individual's Chi.

English:	Warrior
Igbo:	dike
Breakdown:	'di' (being) & 'ike'(strength)
Comments:	A warrior is an embodiment of strength.

Chi, and healing words from an ancient language.

Other Life forms

Insects

English:	Mosquito
Igbo:	Anwụ
Breakdown:	'a' (neutral prefix) & 'nwụ' (die)
Comments:	This word suggests that the ancient Igbo knew that the mosquito carried the deadly malaria parasite. 'a' probably is functioning as the short form of 'anyi' (us).

English:	Ant
Igbo:	Agbusi
Breakdown:	'agbu' (boil, furuncle) & 'si' (stop)
Comments:	These are often the larger ants. They were probably once used to 'treat' a boil. It's possible that there 'jaws' were used to prick open a boil so the contents can discharge. In the Hollywood movie Apocalypto, ants were used to stitch wounds.

English:	Millipedes and similar insects.
Igbo:	ariri
Breakdown:	'a' (negative prefix) & 'ri' (crawl) &' ri' (crawl)
Comments:	These have a tendency to crawl and then stop crawling. As a defense mechanism, they stop crawling and assume a tight coil. This protects their tiny delicate legs from predators.

English:	Termite, small ants
Igbo:	arụrụ
Breakdown:	'a' (negative prefix) 'rụ' (to make) & 'rụ' (to make)
Comments:	These ants can damage or unmake man made wooden structures such as houses while at the same time building their own structures.

Chi, and healing words from an ancient language.

Termites can construct impressive structures.

English:	Grasshopper
Igbo:	ụkpana
Breakdown:	'ụkpa'(scavenger) & 'ana'(land)
Comments:	Grasshopper as scavenger of the land.

Reptiles

English:	Snake
Igbo:	agwọ
Breakdown:	'a' (negative prefix) & 'gwọ' (to heal or make good)
Comments:	Poisonous snakes can deliver a lethal bite. Snakes are not generally associated with health and wellness. In the Biblical account of Adam and Eve, the devil appeared to them in the form of a snake and that brought suffering to humanity.

Chi, and healing words from an ancient language.

English:	Python
Igbo:	Eke
Breakdown:	'e' (prefix used as a partial positive) & 'ke' (to bind)
Comments:	Obviously, what a python does is to 'bind' its prey and suffocate it. Thereafter, the python un-binds before swallowing its meal. The verb 'ke' is also used to denote to 'create'. This is because to 'create' is to 'bind'. A creation is just 'binding' things together.

English:	Chameleon
Igbo:	Ogwumagana
Breakdown:	Ogwu (forest) & 'mụ' (me or my soul) & agana (don't go)
Comments:	This reptile is commonly an inhabitant of deep forests. It hides from predators by assuming the colors of its surroundings. Humans do not have this ability and are vulnerable to predator attacks. Sighting this animal in a forest indicates we are somewhere we shouldn't be. This rule may not apply to game wardens or experienced hunters.

Birds

English:	Wing(of birds)
Igbo:	Nkuku
Breakdown:	'n'(positive prefix) & 'ku' (air movement) and 'ku' (air movement)
Comments:	The wings of a bird are used to create repeated air movements that cause flight.

English:	Vulture
Igbo:	Udene
Breakdown:	'Ude' (prowl-hunt) & 'ene' (watch)
Comments:	That which prowl-hunts and watches.

Chi, and healing words from an ancient language.

A vulture waits for its next meal.

English:	Eagle
Igbo:	Ugo
Breakdown:	'u' (prefix) & 'go' (esteem)
Comments:	This verb is the same in Golibe (be filled with esteem) and ego (money). We notice that the Eagle is a famous icon in many cultures around the world. Evidently, the eagle is a majestic bird that acts with esteem. It tends to nest in very tall trees or high cliffs far away from most predators. Unlike most other birds, the eagle does not make the precautionary 'looking back' before eating its meal. This suggests its well developed self esteem and confidence. In ancient Igbo, many people took Ugo (eagle) titles because they hoped to model their behavior after this confident bird that is full of esteem.

Chi, and healing words from an ancient language.

An Image of an eagle used as part of the facade of a building in New York city.

Mammals

English:	Animal(Wild animal)
Igbo:	Anụ
Breakdown:	'a' & 'nụ'(listen)
Comments:	That which does not listen. Here 'a' also creates the negative. A wild animal cannot listen or obey your command. Distinguish this from domesticated animals not used for food.

Chi, and healing words from an ancient language.

English:	Animal
Igbo:	Anụmana
Breakdown:	'anụ'(meat,flesh/animal), 'ma'(to know) & 'ana'(land)
Comments:	A lower being that knows only the way of the earth or land. Not in tune with God or the heavens.

English:	Lion
Igbo:	ọdụm
Breakdown:	'ọdụ' (advise) & 'mụ' (my soul)
Comments	We notice that the King of Jungle is well respected in many cultures around the world. The lion earns the respect of the lionesses and other beasts out there in the forest. There is majesty in everything it does. That is why the Lion is my counselor. It is the adviser of my soul. Lions served as *advisors* in the thrones of powerful Kings. A lion would instinctively risk 'life or limb' to defend the territory of its lionesses. That's an instinct Kings sought to display when their territory is breached.

English:	Donkey or Horse
Igbo:	Anyinya
Breakdown:	'anyi' (we) & 'nya' (ride)
Comments:	The donkey and the horse were domesticated by humans thousands of years ago. Humans still employ these animals to draw carriages, and in some places they are still used as farm animals. Horses and donkeys played important roles in our earliest civilizations, performing many rigorous tasks humans are unable to achieve. Donkeys and Horses have been 'riding us' for a long time.

Chi, and healing words from an ancient language.

English:	Leopard
Igbo:	Agu
Breakdown:	'a' (negative prefix) & 'gu' (count)
Comments:	When this predator is around we start missing the complete count of sheep, goats and similar animals. This predator usually kills and carts off the animals at night.

English:	Cow
Igbo:	Efi
Breakdown:	'e' (prefix used as a partial negative) & fi (massage, rub)
Comments:	Rubbing or massaging represents a circular-style motion. The curved horns of cattle represent this motion. Further, this animal is not exactly a pet. It is not meant to be massaged or rubbed. They have an unpredictable behavior, and can be temperamental. Fatalities have been recorded. The verb 'fi' is also in 'fia' (rub, massage).

Cattle with their curved horns.

Chi, and healing words from an ancient language.

English:	Horn
Igbo:	Mpi
Breakdown:	'M' (positive prefix) & 'pi' (forward motion)
Comments:	The verb 'pi' is in 'pia' which refers to 'press forward'. The horn is used to 'press forward'. It is useful for offense and defense. In some animals, males spend incredible hours ramming their horns against each other. Fatalities frequently occur, and the winner mates with a horny female. It can be said that the animal with the strongest horn 'presses forward' with its genes.

English:	Goat
Igbo:	Ewu
Breakdown:	'e' (prefix used as a partial positive) & 'wu' (agony). See also nwute (prolonged agony)
Comments:	This animal has a characteristic 'cry' that suggests agony. The goat was one of the earliest animals to be domesticated by man. The goat is very humble and has the look on its face indicating agony. In ancient times, goats were sacrificed to God to atone for our sins so we can be relieved of our agony. Although we have been killing and eating goats for thousands of years; these animals appear ever willing to continue making sacrifices for us. Someone who is stupid is sometimes referred to as a 'goat'. Agony from previous emotionally painful experiences can cause dullness or stupidity.

Food

English:	Soup
Igbo:	Ofe
Breakdown:	'o'(personal prefix) & 'fe' (fly)
Comments:	The idiom 'that doesn't fly' indicates that 'someone does not agree with it'. For example, a woman says; "I love to eat my vegetables raw, but that doesn't fly with my husband". Making a soup is a way to make food items 'fly' (more palatable). Some women believe that the way to a man's heart is through his stomach.

English:	Pumpkin leaves
Igbo:	ụgụ
Breakdown:	'ụ' (community prefix) & 'gụ' (hunger)
Comments:	We all know that one of the major causes of the obesity epidemic is the consumption of excess calories. We have been unwittingly programmed to gobble sugar rich foods and processed carbohydrates. The ancient Igbo was expected to think of green vegetables when hunger sets in. If we can re-set our minds to think of vegetables whenever we feel hungry, that would be quite helpful.

Pumpkin leaves. Image by V Buhl.

Chi, and healing words from an ancient language.

When hunger sets in, the natural response should be vegetables. The NIH recommends that we eat about 8 servings of fruit and vegetables daily.

English:	Melon-seed soup
Igbo:	Egwusi
Breakdown:	"Egwu"(game, play) & "si"(stop)
Comments:	When this soup is ready, it's time for the game (of life) to stop, so we can feed. Egwusi soup is communicating 'timeout'. But after this meal, the game continues.

English:	Bitter leaf Plant
Igbo:	onugbu
Breakdown:	'onu' (bitterness) & 'gbu' (kill)
Comments:	The leaves of this plant are very bitter. They can literally 'kill someone with bitterness'. However, after processing, the leaves can be used to make a lovely enjoyable soup- the bitter leaf soup.

Chi, and healing words from an ancient language.

English:	Yam
Igbo:	Ji
Breakdown:	Ji (hold, holder)
Comments:	Yam is a specialist in converting and storing the energy of the Sun, in the form of complex carbohydrates in its tuber. Yam accomplishes this, in a relatively short period, by utilizing a comparatively thin stem and branches. The carbohydrates in yam are digested slowly by the human body, and the glucose yielded is released gradually into the blood stream over a prolonged period compared to potatoes, rice or other common staples. This is a favorable glycemic index. When an individual eats yam, the energy is prolonged and sustained. Yam is very good for physical and demanding jobs, and in ill patients.

Yam tubers.

Chi, and healing words from an ancient language.

English:	Palm Oil, oil.
Igbo:	Mmanụ.
Breakdown:	Mma (beautiful, knowledge) +nụ (is)
Comments:	Knowledge about oil is very important in creating a beautiful life. Oils are not just important as creams to oil our skins; they are also important food items. The palm oil was so priced, that even the Pharaohs were buried with a portion, for use in the afterlife. Today, evidence is pouring out regarding the benefits of oils(including fish oil) in a wide range of medical conditions. Palm oil is very beautiful oil.

English:	Alcohol
Igbo:	Mmanya.
Breakdown:	'Mma' (beauty) + 'nya' (it)
Comments:	That which is the beauty of it. The beauty of the palm tree is that it can make palm wine (alcohol). The beauty of barley is that we can turn it into beer (alcohol). Alcohol played a key role in the earliest human civilizations. Be careful when you drink alcohol because it distorts realty and make things more beautiful than they seem.

English:	Cassava (meal)
Igbo:	Akpụ
Breakdown:	'a' (negative prefix) and 'kpụ' (mold)
Comments:	'Kpụ' is something molded and strong. This verb is found in the word for bone (ọkpụkpụ). It appears as if akpụ refers to the finished cassava meal which is relatively soft and easy to mold into different shapes, hence the term 'unmolded'. They may also be referring, in addition, to the cassava plant itself. This plant has very tough looking erect stem that is relatively easy to break.

Chi, and healing words from an ancient language.

English:	Cook
Igbo:	Si
Breakdown:	si=reinforce or strengthen
Comments:	Cooking is a way to reinforce different food ingredients together. It also breaks down food items so nutrients are available for digestion.

English:	Tree
Igbo:	Osisi
Breakdown:	'O' (prefix) & 'si' (strengthen) & 'si' (strengthen)
Comments:	A tree represents strength. A tree plays many ecological roles such as strengthening the earth and protecting it from erosion. A tree also protects communities from fierce winds and storms due to its strength. They are soldiers we often take for granted. Trees also provide the strong materials we use to build houses, furniture and other sundry items. In the Igbo word tree, 'osisi' is carried by the same branch as 'si' which is cook. Cooking is basically strengthening food. These words are also carried by the same branch because the firewood which cooking depended on, comes from trees. This is a good example of synergism.

Cut tree that could be used for firewood.

Chi, and healing words from an ancient language.

English:	Igbo apple
Igbo:	ụdala
Breakdown:	'ụda'(to fall)& and 'la' (lick)
Comments:	When this exotic fruit falls, it is time to pick it up and lick or suck its delicious innards.

English:	Banana
Igbo:	Unere.
Breakdown:	'unọ'(house)& 'ere'(to leak)
Comments:	Banana leaves can be used to fix roof leaks.

English:	Eat
Igbo:	Ri
Breakdown:	'Ri'=flow
Comments:	This verb is also found in the word for water (mmiri). To eat food is to 'flow' food. Food 'flows' from one organism to another. Lower life forms support higher life forms. For example, the much regarded omega 3 fish oils are not made by fish. Fish get them by ingesting algae in water.

English:	Bitter
Igbo:	Inu
Breakdown:	'I' (strong positive prefix) & 'nu'(bitter)
Comments:	Bitter appears to be a strong form of the salty taste. See salt (nnu)

English:	Salt
Igbo:	Nnu
Breakdown:	'N'(positive prefix) & 'nu' (bitter)
Comments:	Apparently they considered salty taste as a mild variant of bitterness. While ion channels regulate the salt sensation in humans, a different set of regulators govern bitter taste.

Chi, and healing words from an ancient language.

Human disasters

English:	War
Igbo:	Agha
Breakdown:	'a' (negative prefix) & 'gha' (spread, disperse)= lack of spreading or contraction.
Comments:	Some people consider war a necessary evil. War has been a feature of human life for thousands of years. War causes human suffering on and indescribable scale, yet man continues to war. In World War II alone, over 60 million people representing more than 2.5% of the human population perished. The Germans and the Russians suffered much heavier casualties. Historians write volumes on the causes of war, but the creators of Igbo consider it due to 'spread'. War is caused by the wild 'spreading' of people and their spiritual and physical activities. A war (aqha) causes the opposite-contraction. During the Biafran war, it is estimated that over 1 million civilian and military deaths occurred. In an effort to support the war effort, communities were required to supply young males for the Biafran effort. Many never came back, their bodies were never found, and families were never compensated.

Starving woman during the Nigerian-Biafran war. Over 1 million people perished.

Chi, and healing words from an ancient language.

English:	Hunger
Igbo:	Agụlụ
Breakdown:	'a'(negative prefix) & 'gụlụ'(to count)
Comments:	Living in a context of lack (spiritual and physical). A person who is hungry has nothing to count. No food stock or live-stock or money to count. This individual has nothing to count on. One way of preventing hunger or scarcity is to keep an accurate count of your possessions. This is a way to master your possessions, so you can cause them to increase.

Igbo management and leadership structure.

English:	Eri (name of Igbo Spiritual Leader)
Igbo:	Eri
Breakdown:	'e' & 'ri'(leak, flow or reach out)
Comments:	'e'-creates a partial positive- This is a spiritual leader who causes the gentle flow of love and other spiritually related materials. See also Nri (town and civilization headquarters). According to Igbo history, Eri is a sky being. It is not clear if he was an extra-terrestrial or if he was delivered to earth from a spaceship.

English:	Nri (Igbo Kingdom)
Igbo:	Nri
Breakdown:	'N'(positive prefix) & 'ri'(to reach out, leak out, or flow)
Comments:	Living in a context of the need for spiritual food. Nri was created to lighten the burden of mankind through spiritual techniques just like Christianity. Nri was also advanced in farming techniques, and in ancient times was an agricultural research and development site. Nri developed and delivered spiritual techniques that 'flowed' around Igbo land and neighboring states.

Chi, and healing words from an ancient language.

English:	King
Igbo:	Eze
Breakdown:	'E' (partial positive) & 'ze' (shield, guard)
Comments:	The king is the shield of the community. The verb 'ze' is also seen in the lower level priests called Nze. The use of 'e' rather than 'n' suggests that the Nze have a stronger role protecting and guiding the masses compared to the King 'Eze'. The Nze were more in contact with the people in their day to day activities. The King is not directly involved in 'shepherding' the average person. The Nze were the go between in matters requiring the attention of the King. In such cases, they need to liaise with the higher level Ozo Priests which are much fewer in number. Nze priests are trained by Ozo priests. This is a pyramidal system with the King on top, then Ozo priests, followed by Nze priests, and finally the people. The verb in Ozo is 'zo' which means to 'save'. Substitution of 'o' by 'e' yields a similar verb 'ze' in Eze which denotes 'guarding'. This is an illustration of the deliberate engineering of sounds to yield related actions. It is obvious that 'protection' or 'guarding' is a strong theme in the management of the Igbo people. The very word Igbo means 'guard'. The Igbo (people) were mainly an agricultural society which is called Ugbo(farming) with the verb gbo meaning to 'guard'. Farming (Ugbo) was a way to guard against hunger and scarcity. We can readily observe a perfect alignment of purpose between a people, their work and their leadership under the theme 'guarding'. In order for their aspiration to come to fruition, there must be love. We know from 1 Corinthians Chapter 13 vs. 7-8 that love always protects (guards), and it never fails.

Chi, and healing words from an ancient language.

King
(Eze)
Ozo (Savior
priest)
Nze (shepherd
priests)
The People

English:	Saviour Priest (Ozo)
Igbo:	ọzọ
Breakdown:	'ọ'(prefix) & 'zọ' (to save)
Comments:	High priest who saves. These priests were designed to counsel the King and report to the King.

English:	Shepherd Priest.
Igbo:	Nze
Breakdown:	'N' & ' ze' (to protect)
Comments:	Lower level priest serves as a protector, guardian or shepherd of the masses. They are trained by ọzọ priests and deal directly with the people. In communities were Nzes are active, they are individuals you go to when you need a favor.

Chi, and healing words from an ancient language.

English:	Igbo(people)
Igbo:	Igbo
Breakdown:	'I' (strong positive prefix) & 'gbo' (prevent, protect, guard)
Comments:	I is an intensifier. An Igbo is a Guard. What are they guarding? See also Ugbo (farming) To be Igbo, is to live a protected life. Protected by God, the leadership, and a witness to the protection.

Prof. Chinua Achebe, the famous author of "Things fall apart"; is an Igbo writer. Image by Stuart Shapiro

English:	House (central house)
Igbo:	Obi
Breakdown:	'O' & 'bi' (to live, to be alive) 'O' is an intensifier used in personal terms.
Comments:	The house of a man is called an Obi. It is like the heart of the family unit. A man directs his life, and that of his family, from the Obi.

Chi, and healing words from an ancient language.

English:	Position (powerful position)
Igbo:	okwa
Breakdown:	'o' (personal prefix) & ' kwa' (cry)
Comments:	A position represents a deep spiritual responsibility. People get positions because they are needed to solve problems for society. A person in any good position quickly learns to communicate the problems to all concerned while seeking solutions. This is done through 'weeping'. A cry is a communication of urgency. When a baby cries, caregivers are motivated to take action. This is even more powerful when an adult cries. This does not mean the person in a position should be weeping. It only means they should communicate with deep compassion. A 'cry' also represents humility.

English:	Title
Igbo:	tu
Breakdown:	tu (oneness) see from the number one (otu)
Comments:	The purpose of a title is to create oneness between an individual and the title. For example, an individual whose title is 'Lion' is trying to achieve oneness with a lion. The goal is to act like a Lion.

English:	Lion
Igbo:	ọdụm
Breakdown:	'ọdụ' (advise) & 'mụ' (my soul)
Comments	We readily notice that the King of Jungle is well respected in many cultures around the world. The lion earns the respect of the lionesses and other beasts out there in the forest. There is majesty in everything it does. That is why the Lion is my counselor. It is the adviser of my soul. Lions served as *advisors* in the thrones of powerful Kings. A lion would instinctively risk 'life or limb' to defend the territory of its lionesses. That's an instinct Kings sought to display when their territory is breached.

Chi, and healing words from an ancient language.

Imperial coat of arms of Ethiopia under Menelik II. Note the throne of Solomon and the Lion of Judah. Courtesy Tom Lemmens.

Igbo leadership structure

The verb 'gbo' which means guard is seen in ugbo (farm) and Igbo (the people). The Igbo people were an agricultural society. Farming guards against hunger and other society problems.

The verb 'ze' which means 'protect' is seen in Eze (King) and Nze (Shepherd priest). The King and the Nze are the leaders of the people. We can readily note a strong theme of guarding and protection in Igbo life and leadership.

This is a very good example of synergism, or alignment of purpose. The people are motivated to guard their Chi and their livelihood.

Chi, and healing words from an ancient language.

Names

English:	Name
Igbo:	Afa
Breakdown:	' a' (negative prefix)& 'fa' (them)
Comments:	The name of an individual is unique, and separates the individual from other members of the community. A name is important in the sense that it helps individuals fashion and develop a way of being. It would be awkward for someone named Moses to be an enslaver of people.

English:	Ada(name)
Igbo:	Ada
Breakdown:	'a' (negative prefix) & 'da'(fall)
Comments:	Name given to first daughter. Prevents the fall of the family. Prevents the fall of the Obi (house) as in Adaobi. The action of the first daughter is to prevent the fall of her fathers and husbands household. This places plenty of responsibility on the shoulders of first daughters.

English:	Chioma (name)
Igbo:	Chiọma
Breakdown:	'Chi' (personal emotional force) & 'ọma' (good)
Comments:	This indicates someone with a good Chi. It is a common female name.

Chi, and healing words from an ancient language.

English:	Afulenu(name)
Igbo:	Afuluenu
Breakdown:	'afulu' (seen) & 'enu' (sky)
Comments:	When a beautiful child comes into the family, you might consider this name. 'we have seen the sky' is a way to acknowledge that God has given us part of his majesty and glamour.

English:	Ojukwu (name).
Igbo:	Ojukwu
Breakdown:	'Oju' (filled up) & 'ukwu' (big, a lot, plenty)
Comments:	The bearer of this name is a stand for abundance. He is a means for abundance in his community.

English:	Nwosu(name)
Igbo:	Nwosu
Breakdown:	Nwa (son) and osu (an ancient deity that can invoke the ancestors)
Comments;	This is a descendant of a deity that can invoke the ancestors.

Chi, and healing words from an ancient language.

<u>CONCLUSION</u>

Africa is well known for its human and material resources. Ancient African civilizations, such as Ancient Egypt, left us monuments that still amaze us till this day. Many of those monuments played critical life defining roles in those civilizations. We can assume that those structures were disabled at some time in history following the fall of those civilizations. The new leaders imposed rival systems that rendered the 'monuments' obsolete.

In the same vein, we can consider that, Igbo was disabled at some point in history. What we use Igbo for today can be compared to what we use the Pyramids of Giza for today.

The Chi is a spiritual and emotional complex that, under normal circumstances, should contain love, joy, happiness and other positive emotions. When it contains sadness, despair, jealousy and other negative emotions, misfortune is bound to arise. Individuals should be conscious of the state of their chi, so proper adjustments can be made when necessary.

 Igbo words are practical and are designed to help an individual gain competence in their universe. I hope you found this work useful. The writer does not believe this is the final or complete guide to the understanding of Igbo words. The writer hopes this will stimulate interest in the Igbo language and the embedded technology. It is believed that understanding these words would help individuals gain and apply more wisdom.

Since knowledge is power, and power is creation, I hope this book would boost your creativity. Although sub-Saharan Africa is considered the poorest area of the world, this book suggests the astounding creative talent of the Igbo ancestors. I believe this will boost the esteem of Africans and their descendants, as well as humanity in general.

This book is also intended to deal a blow to the theory of Afro-pessimism.

Chi, and healing words from an ancient language.

I recommend that you read the book several times so you can draw your own conclusions. Many of the words convey very complex information that was deliberately shortened to make the book readable by a wide audience.

Hopefully, this book helped shift your understanding of the universe a little bit.

Chi, and healing words from an ancient language.

<u>THE END</u>

Chi, and healing words from an ancient language.

BIBLIOGRAPHY

1. Aguwa, Jude C. U. (1995). *The Agwu deity in Igbo religion*. Fourth Dimension Publishing Co., Ltd. p. 29. ISBN 978-156-399-0.
2. Basden, George Thomas (1921). *Among the Ibos of Nigeria.* Nonsuch Publishing
3. Botha, R. and C. Knight (eds) 2009. *The Cradle of Language.* Oxford: Oxford University Press.
4. Chikodi Anunobi. Nri Warriors of Peace. Zenith Press; 1 edition (February 28, 2006)
5. Chinua Achebe. Things Fall Apart. Anchor Books -- Doubleday, NYC (January 1, 1994)
6. Chinua Achebe. No Longer at Ease. Heinemann, 1960.
7. Chinua Achebe. Arrow of God. Heinemann, 1964.
8. Christopher Ejizu. Ofo; Igbo ritual and symbol. Fourth Dimension Publishing Co. (March 11, 2002).
9. Dr. Creflo Dollar. Experiencing God's Love. A guide for new believers. Creflo Dollar Ministries ISBN 1-59089-806-0.
10. Eckhart Tolle. The Power of Now: A Guide to Spiritual Enlightenment. New world library, 2004
11. Eckhart Tolle. A New Earth. Awakening to your Life's purpose. Penguin, 2008.
12. Frantzis, Bruce Kumar . *The Chi Revolution: Harnessing the Healing Power of Your Life Force*. Blue Snake Books. ISBN 1-58394-193-2.
13. Holt, Stephen. Combat Syndrom X, Y, Z. Wellness publishing (2002).
14. http://en.wikipedia.org/wiki/Shalom
15. Ilogu, Edmund (1974). *Christianity and Ibo culture*. Brill. ISBN 90-04-04021-8
16. Isichei, Elizabeth Allo (1997). *A History of African Societies to 1870*. Cambridge University Press. p. 247. ISBN 0-521-45599-5.
17. Iwu, Maurice. *Handbook of African medicinal plants*. CRC Press; 1 edition (February 18, 1993)
18. M. O. Ené "The fundamentals of Odinani",
19. http://www.kwenu.com/odinani/odinani.htm
20. Ogomaka, P.M.C, (in press), 'Number Systems including some Indigenous Number Systems'. Teaching Modules for Secondary School Teachers of General Mathematics, Abuja: NMC

Chi, and healing words from an ancient language.
21. Ogomaka, P.M.C. & Akukwe, A.C., 1998, 'School and Work place Mathematics in Imo State: Some implications', Nigerian Journal of Curriculum and Instruction, Vol. 7, No 1:13-18
22. Ohuche, R.O, Ezeilo, J.O.C; Eke, B. I, et al., 1986, Everyday Mathematics for the Junior Secondary School, Book 1, Enugu: Fourth Dimension Publishers.
23. Olaudah Equiano, *The Interesting Narrative of the Life of Olaudah Equiano, or Gustavus Vassa, the African.* Simon & Brown publishers.
24. Onwuejeogwu, M. Angulu (1981). *An Igbo civilization: Nri kingdom & hegemony*. Ethnographica. ISBN 978-123-105-X.
25. Opata, Damian U. Ekwensu In the Igbo Imagination : a Heroic Deity Or Christian Devil, Nsukka, Nigeria : Great AP Express, 2005.
26. Pamela J. W. Gore (1996-01-22). "Phases of the Moon". Georgia Perimeter College. http://facstaff.gpc.edu/~pgore/astronomy/astr101/moonphas.htm
27. Patrick Mathias Chukwuaku Ogomaka. Traditional Igbo Numbering System: A Reconstruction. Africa Development, Vol. XXX, No.3, 2005, pp. 35–47 © Council for the Development of Social Science Research in Africa, 2005 (ISSN 0850-3907)
28. Richard P. Brown M.D. and Patricia L. Gerbarg. The Healing Power of the breath. 2012 Shambhala publications.
29. Sylvester Okwunodu Ogbechie,: *Ben Enwonwu: the making of an African modernist*, page 161. University Rochester Press, 2008.
30. The Holy Bible.
31. Uchendu, Victor C. *The Igbo of Southeast Nigeria*. Van Nostrand Reinhold Company, 1965

32. Udeani, Chibueze C. (2007). *Inculturation as dialogue: Igbo culture and the message of Christ*. Rodopi. p. 28—29. ISBN 90-420-2229-9.
33. Uzukwu, E. Elochukwu (1997). *Worship as body language: introduction to Christian worship : an African orientation*. Liturgical Press. ISBN 0-8146-6151-3.

Chi, and healing words from an ancient language.

<u>ABOUT THE AUTHOR</u>

Dr. Uzoma Nwosu is a graduate of College of Medicine, University of Nigeria, Enugu Campus. He worked as a Principal Medical Officer with the department of Health, Johannesburg, South Africa before joining the Pharmaceutical Industry to perform research. Dr. Nwosu also worked as a Research Fellow at the NYU Hospital for Joint Diseases. He is a co-author of peer-reviewed medical papers.

He is keenly interested in African culture, and its impact on human health and development. The decision to write this book was made after reading the book "Nri Warriors of Peace" by Chikodi Anunobi. Subsequently, an analysis of the Igbo word for lungs, 'ngugu' showed it was coined from the verb 'gugu' which means to console. This discovery led to Dr. Richard Brown and his wife Dr. Patricia Garberg, who teach the use of breath in Healing.

This helped validate the many thoughts behind Igbo words and accelerated the development of this book.

Chi, and healing words from an ancient language.

INDEX AND NOTES

Chi, and healing words from an ancient language.

Chi, and healing words from an ancient language.

Chi, and healing words from an ancient language.

Chi, and healing words from an ancient language.

Chi, and healing words from an ancient language.

Chi, and healing words from an ancient language.

Chi, and healing words from an ancient language.

Chi, and healing words from an ancient language.

Chi, and healing words from an ancient language.

www.ingramcontent.com/pod-product-compliance
Lightning Source LLC
Chambersburg PA
CBHW061319110426
42742CB00012BA/2250